THE DISAPPOINTMENT,

OR, THE FORCE OF CREDULITY

The Disappointment,
or, the Force of Credulity

by A N D R E W   B A R T O N
(Pseudonym of Thomas Forrest)

A Critical Edition
of the First American Drama
Edited and Annotated by

D A V I D   M A Y S

A Florida Technological University Book

THE UNIVERSITY PRESSES OF FLORIDA

Gainesville · 1976

Library of Congress Cataloging in Publication Data

Barton, Andrew, pseud.
  The disappointment.

  Also attributed to John Leacock.
  "A Florida Technological University book."
  Bibliography: p.
  I. Leacock, John. II. Title.
PS707.B2D5 1976   812'.2   76–26470
ISBN 0–8130–0562–0

Designed by Gary Gore

Typography by Modern Typographers, Inc., Clearwater, Florida
Printed by Storter Printing Company, Gainesville, Florida

For

Anne Devall Mays,

Ann Tournier Mays,

and

Monroe Lippman.

ACKNOWLEDGMENTS

A number of people have offered valuable aid and advice in the preparation of this edition. Professor Roland Browne of the English Department of Florida Technological University offered unstinting editorial help and moral support, as did Mrs. Shirley Boutwell, who accepted the burden of typing the manuscript. Dr. Charles N. Micarelli, dean of the College of Humanities and Fine Arts, Florida Technological University, offered constant support, both tangible and intangible. Dr. Harry W. Smith, acting chairman of the Department of Theater, Florida Technological University, read the manuscript with a hard critical awareness. I am indebted to Dr. Paul S. Hostetler of the University of Washington for making several important corrections. I thank each of the many people who contributed constructive critical advice. If this edition possesses any virtues it is in large measure due to them, and any faults or errors it may contain are mine, not theirs.

Father John Bluett of St. Margaret Mary Church in Winter Park, Florida, graciously offered his Irish background to interpret many of the phrases used by Trushoop in the play, as well as his knowledge of Latin to decipher Rattletrap's incantations. I am very grateful to him and to his staff for their help.

Dr. Paul Wehr of the Florida Technological University History Department provided me with a great deal of helpful information about colonial American history. The reference staff of the university library received my questions and frequent requests with unwavering professionalism. I am grateful for their patience and assistance.

Lastly, I must thank my children, Christopher, Ann Maury, Matthew, and Suzannah, for enduring with their father during the time he spent in the eighteenth century.

Contents

Introduction

The Event

In April of 1767 the American Company of Comedians announced the forthcoming production of a new comic opera, *The Disappointment, or The Force of Credulity*, in its new theater near Philadelphia, the Southwark. Two days before its opening, the *Pennsylvania Gazette* tersely announced that " 'The Disappointment' (that was advertised for Monday), as it contains personal reflections, is unfit for the stage." A standard in the eighteenth-century repertoire, Congreve's *The Mourning Bride*, was substituted. Six days after the withdrawal of *The Disappointment*, on April 24, 1767, Thomas Godfrey's *The Prince of Parthia* was performed, thus gaining the place in American theater that *The Disappointment* had been denied, the historical distinction of being the first play written by an American to enjoy professional production on this continent.[1]

This decision by David Douglass, the manager of the American Company, doomed *The Disappointment* to almost total obscurity. While the play was published in New York in the same year, it has never been performed. A revision of the play some twenty-nine years later did nothing to revive it for the stage, and *The Disappointment*, ominously named, has remained a bit of dramatic curiosa until the present day.

This state of affairs is unfortunate, for *The Disappointment* is a play that repays reading and study, if not production. The play itself, as well as the social and political circumstances that surround its cancellation, can tell us much about the society that created it. Furthermore, the work is interesting in its own right, in that it contains several elements that were later to become staples of the American dramatic form. It is comic, satiric without being biting, socially oriented, filled with local color and ethnic characters, infused with a positive thematic morality, and purposeful in intent. Each of these qualities, in varying degree, has been present in all successful American comedies, from Tyler to Simon, and their presence is interestingly foreshadowed in *The Disappointment*. While certainly no masterpiece, *The Disappointment* does possess the

1

theatrical virtue of being funny and lively, written by a young man with a good eye and ear for what would amuse his particular audience. The characters are clearly, if broadly, drawn, and occasionally "something very much like wit" illuminates them. The play, as a theatrical work, has a genial air about it that is endearing.

With this, the play's curtailed production history can afford us a number of valuable insights into the social activities and attitudes of the pre-Revolutionary period, as well as illustrate the precarious state of the dramatic arts in North America at that time. The theater had many opponents in colonial America, particularly among religious leaders, but *The Disappointment* succumbed to a combination of pressures that were only in part prompted by religious conservatism. A curious amalgam of forces (a number of them imagined by Douglass) affected the withdrawal of *The Disappointment*—some personal, some political, and many self-serving.

Other aspects of *The Disappointment* may also be of interest. There was no such person as Andrew Barton. The actual authorship of the play has been questioned, and this problem has implications that are much more important than the mere attribution of a minor literary work to the correct amateur. Although crude in its construction, *The Disappointment* shows the hand of someone well-versed in eighteenth-century theatrical production, if only in its workmanlike stage directions. Furthermore, the form of the play, while faulty, does contain many comic aspects: a clear, if repetitive, exposition; rising action and complications; characters that are consistent and simply motivated; and the traditional comic "happy idea," *agons* and *kommos*. This is not to imply that the work is Aristophanic in its quality, but *The Disappointment* does possess certain characteristics of comedy that reveal the author to be something more than a dilettante.

The ethnic figures in the work deserve some attention as well. The author has provided us with a Scots, an Irishman, and a character that several commentators on the work have described as a German or, more interestingly, as a Negro. If the character of Raccoon is intended to be the latter, *The Disappointment* gains in historical importance as the vehicle that would first portray the American black on the stage.

Lastly, *The Disappointment* provides us with a delightful example of eighteenth-century popular drama, with many of the characteristic qualities of that fascinating and contradictory period. On one level, the work may be seen as a mundane application of the period's intellectual interest in rationality and common sense; on another, it is representative of the Age of Reason's frank and healthy interest in and awareness of human frailties and desires, particularly in sexual matters. There is an openness about the comic relationships of Raccoon, Moll Placket, and the sailor Topinlift that, while condemned as licentious by nineteenth-century historians and critics, can only be described as refreshing by modern readers.

Thus, *The Disappointment* is of value in a number of areas—historical, cultural, theatrical, and literary. It is a fascinating artifact of our dramatic and social past that deserves recognition.

The Production History

The precipitate withdrawal of *The Disappointment* from performance represented a theatrical defeat of some proportions for the American Company of Comedians in their constant struggle against the repressive social elements that surrounded them. It is perhaps important that the circumstances that brought about the cancellation be determined, insofar as it is possible to do so.

The would-be producer of *The Disappointment* was David Douglass, manager of the American Company of Comedians and second husband to Mrs. Lewis Hallam, widow of the first truly professional theater manager in North America. Douglass, a fascinating figure in his own right, had been an actor-manager in Jamaica and the West Indies for several years before the Hallam Troupe visited there in 1756. Lewis Hallam died in Jamaica that year, and Douglass amalgamated the two acting companies personally and professionally by marrying the widowed Mrs. Hallam in that same year.

In 1758, encouraged by his wife and the members of the company, Douglass made his first foray into North America. It is beyond the scope of this work to detail the manifold problems and stratagems that made the task of theatrical production so difficult in colonial North America; it is enough to say that Douglass was faced with a bewildering variety of religious objections, moral fulminations, legal maneuvers, and political dealings to be overcome in virtually every city to which he took the company. It is a tribute to his skill at public relations and his dedication to the cause of professional theater that he was able to conquer many of the objections and pitfalls that would, if it had been possible, have denied the theater to this hemisphere.

It seemed that the antitheatrical forces were most varied and impassioned in Philadelphia. To begin with, the Quakers had established a position against the theater, best summarized by their leader in America, William Penn, who asked rhetorically in *No Cross, No Crown,* "How many plays did Jesus Christ and his apostles recreate themself at?" To the Quaker the theater was inextricably involved with those repressive and libertine forces that had caused them to flee England less than a century before. Lewis Hallam's first venture into Philadelphia in 1754 had touched off a barrage of diatribe against the theater as "the Temple of Satan," culminating in a petition (the first of many) to the governor of the province requesting an injunction against the players. The governor, James Hamilton, refused the petition and permitted the players to perform thirty plays, but the Quakers, now allied with a large and noisy Presbyterian faction, were not finished. On the occasion of Douglass's first visit to Philadelphia, in 1758, the religious conservatives again petitioned the government to deny him permission to play. The ruling, handed down by one Judge Allan, was (in the words of John Watson, annalist of the period) "repulsive, saying he got more moral virtue from plays than from sermons."

Despite these rebuffs, religious opposition to the theater in the City of Brotherly Love remained a constant force to be simultaneously placated and defied by Douglass in the pursuit of his artistic and professional ends.

In the late 1760s another source of opposition developed—the political nativists known loosely as the Sons of Liberty. The passage of the Stamp Act and its subsequent enforcement had inflamed the North American colonies as had few other legislative measures of the British Parliament. Riots, pamphlets, threats, and mob violence filled the air, and many of the ignorant protesters looked upon the theater as a tangible object of British oppression. Douglass was aware of this early manifestation of American anti-intellectualism, and did much to stress the somewhat dubious "Americanness" of his actors and their profession. It was at this time that the name of the company was changed from the London Company to the American Company, in what was obviously a naïve attempt to downplay the origins of the group.[2]

These ploys were unsuccessful, particularly in one painful instance. On the fifth of May, 1766, a mob destroyed the Chapel Street theater, the New York home of the American Company. Details of the riot are scanty, particularly regarding its cause, but the effects were devastating. The theater was totally demolished, and portions of it were taken to a large public square and burned. Odell, whose *Annals of the New York*

Stage may be considered definitive, believed that "the Sons of Liberty
. . . were probably instrumental in the demolition of the theatre." As
for the cause, Odell says, with a fatalistic shrug, ". . . (the actors) were
English, and that was enough for the Sons of Liberty."[3]

While the Sons of Liberty were not as demonstrative in Philadelphia
as in New York, they were still a power with which Douglass had to be
prepared to contend if it became necessary. We do know that the Philadelphia mob demonstrated against the Stamp Act, the chief source of
irritation for the Sons of Liberty, and felt sufficiently bold to threaten
Benjamin Franklin's home and wife for his suspected compliance with
the hated legislation. These demonstrations took place in early September 1766, and the potential force of the Philadelphia mob must have
been known to Douglass.[4]

A third source of opposition to the theater came from the middle
class, particularly in Philadelphia. The Bridenbaughs observe: "Many
of the thrifty middle class—carpenters, masons, and tailors—resented
the ostentatious gentility of the theatre, quite as much as, in their capac-
ities of Quaker, Baptist, or Presbyterian, they deplored its supposed
effect on morality and religion. By the eve of the Revolution this secu-
larization of anti-stage feeling was complete, and opposition to the
theatre had become almost wholly social and economic."[5]

Thus it was that *The Disappointment*, or any play for that matter,
faced opposition from any one of three sources: religious, political, or
economic. The successful censoring of *The Disappointment* came from
the economic element.

The probable author of the work based his play upon what is
thought to have been an elaborate practical joke that he and several
of his friends played upon certain credulous *petit bourgeois* in Philadelphia. A contemporary letter tells us that the butts of the joke in the play
were in reality Richard Swan, a prominent hatter, a barber named
Dixon, and an Irish cooper and Scotch tailor, both nameless. The letter
writer, John MacPherson, states: "This play was never acted before,
the opposition to it being so great as not to admit of it. Raccoon (i.e.
Swan the hatter) swore that it might begin a Comedy, but that he would
make it end in a Tragedy."

John Fanning Watson, the indefatigable compiler of *Annals of Philadelphia and Pennsylvania* . . . , adds that Anthony Armbruster, a local
printer, was involved in the original joke as one of the dupes, and that
he joined with Swan in objecting to the public humiliation that theatri-

cal production would bring upon them. So, as the announcement of impending production was made, it seems certain that these two men presented their objections to Douglass.

It should be remembered that the actual author of *The Disappointment*—if it was Thomas Forrest, writing under the pen name Andrew Barton—had several powerful points of argument on his side in favor of the production. Forrest was a member of a socially prominent group of young men that included "Mad" Anthony Wayne, the schoolmaster John Reily, and the before-mentioned John MacPherson. Surely these men, educated citizens of some importance, could have outweighed the objections raised by a hatter and an obscure printer. This would doubtless have been the case had it not been for the fact that Swan and several others connected with the original joke were members of the local and powerful Order of Freemasons, in common with David Douglass, the producer.[6]

Douglass depended upon the Masons to a remarkable extent for the survival of his theatrical enterprises. Hugh Rankin has commented on the "relationship between the theatre and the fraternal order of Masons that remained constant throughout the colonial period," a relationship that Douglass more than any other developed and maintained. He was given to speaking the prologues to his production "in the character of a Master Mason," and performed to order for the fraternity at every opportunity. Many of the "benefits"—those performances from which the proceeds were given to one member of the company—were supported by the Masonic lodges in a number of cities.

That Douglass depended upon the various Masonic lodges in the cities in which he performed is a fact without question. It follows that he would be extremely reluctant to antagonize his brothers by not giving in to their objections. Moreover, Douglass was acutely aware of the power of an aroused mob, remembering as he must have the Chapel Street disaster only thirteen months before. Swan's remark that the play, if presented, "would end in a Tragedy" could be taken as a direct threat, and Douglass undoubtedly conceded to Swan and Armbruster's demands.[7]

Armbruster's role in the matter is less well-defined. MacPherson does not mention him as one of the victims of the satire, nor is there a character in the piece to equate with a German printer. There is a reference in Watson to the fact that Armbruster was one of the dupes in the original joke, and perhaps the printer felt that public production of the work based on his humiliating experience might remind the citizens of Philadelphia and reopen old wounds. Furthermore, Armbruster was proud of his reputation as an almanac-maker, and the joking references to the "High-Dutch" almanac used by Moll Placket to distract Raccoon in Act II, scene i, may have offended the printer. Moll does make reference to her uncle—characterizing him as a hex-doctor in Germantown, *au courant* with spells, witchcraft, and magic, and the author of the almanac—and as Armbruster had a reputation as a dabbler in the occult, it is not beyond reason that he saw himself maligned in the play as a foolish adept and the uncle of a whore.[8]

It is highly unlikely that we shall ever know the exact circumstances that surround Douglass's decision to withdraw *The Disappointment* from production, but it is reasonable to speculate from the known facts that it may well have been based upon the above consideration. Descriptions of Douglass's character and of his devotion to the continuation of the professional theater support the plausibility of this conjecture.

Douglass may be faulted for his failure to stand up for artistic freedom, but the exigencies of professional production in colonial America demanded that he deny himself the luxury of that philosophic posture. Besides, it was not in Douglass's character to place an abstract concept before a political reality. His main concern seemed to be social acceptance, expressed in that timeless quantifier, the box office, and if he had to compromise and adapt to circumstance he seemed willing to do so. We know, for example, that he was quite willing to emphasize certain elements in his productions that would bid fair to please the particular audience that he wished to attract. He was not above presenting *Douglas* in Philadelphia as a moral tract, making certain that the advertisements mentioned that the play was "written by the Rev. Mr. Hume [sic], a Minister of the Kirk of Scotland." The religious conservatives of Rhode Island were presumably attracted to his production of *Othello* when it was billed as "a series of Moral Dialogues in Five Parts, Depicting the Evil Effects of Jealousy and other Bad Passions, and Proving that Happiness can only Spring from the Pursuit of Virtue."[9]

It seems obvious that Douglass put professional survival above artistic exactitude. His dedication to the theater was immense, if measured only in terms of what he did to insure its continued existence. His was the only professional company of performers on the North American continent, and it seems certain that he was aware of its historical importance. This awareness, coupled with the instinct of a good businessman, must have led him to the conclusion that *The Disappointment*'s production would do more harm than good to the American Company's reputation.

Much the same professional reasoning prompted Douglass's decision to produce *The Disappointment* in the first place. He realized that local dramatic talent should and must be encouraged, for both its immediate and long-range benefits; and, if the Author's Preface to the published play may be believed, there was definite public pressure on Douglass for the theatrical production of the practical joke that had amused the city for some time. Douglass, in the tradition of the showman, must have realized the publicity value of local talent, particularly in Philadelphia, for he rushed to acquire and produce *The Prince of Parthia*, by another young Philadelphian, Thomas Godfrey.

His theatrical instincts betrayed him in this case, however, as *The Prince of Parthia* was a palpable failure, surviving only one professional performance. As a partisan of *The Disappointment*, I believe that the comedy would have had a greater chance of success than the turgid, derivative tragedy performed in its place—but that, of course, is speculation.[10] Douglass's motives in accepting *The Disappointment* for production were not of the highest order: he obviously felt the chief merit of the work lay in its local sensationalism. It is ironic that it was cancelled for the same reason that first appealed to its would-be producer.

The Author

Critics and historians propose two candidates for the authorship of *The Disappointment*: John Leacock and Thomas Forrest. Neither of these men claimed the right to be called the author of the play; Leacock was suggested by an early historian of the theater in America, and Forrest is considered the author by traditional consensus. I hold the opinion that Forrest's is the stronger claim. The entire matter would be superbly moot were it not for the fact that *The Disappointment* has some real cultural and historical value; if proper credit for its creation can be given, it is only just to do so.

The advocates of Leacock base their case upon two elements, one objective and probably inaccurate, the other subjective and inexplicable. In the first instance, Leacock is listed as the author of *Disappointed*, published in Philadelphia in 1796, in a book by William Dunlap, "Father of the American Theater" and its first historian. Dunlap cites Leacock in an appendix to his seminal work *History of the American*

Theatre and Anecdotes of the Principal Actors (1832) and, confusingly, lists "Andrew Barton" elsewhere as the author of *The Disappointment*. No other reference to either Leacock or "Barton" appear in Dunlap's fascinating and imaginative work.

It seems obvious that Dunlap was simply misinformed about Leacock, and it is equally apparent that he never saw a copy of the work attributed to the man. If he had, he certainly would have listed the title correctly and made certain that the author of record was the same one listed earlier in the appendix. Furthermore, Dunlap's *Disappointed* is quite obviously the second edition of *The Disappointment*, printed in Philadelphia in 1796. The basis on which this work was ascribed to Leacock is impossible to determine. However, William Dunlap's place in American theater history is secure, and it does him no discredit to suggest that in this instance his research was faulty.

Leacock is credited with writing one play, *The Fall of British Tyranny* in 1776, although this attribution is not without its own confusion. There is some mention of Joseph Leacock, a Philadelphia silversmith, as the author of this Revolutionary War propaganda piece, but the weight of opinion seems to favor John Leacock, at one time the coroner of Philadelphia. Whatever the merits of John Leacock's case as the author of *The Fall of British Tyranny*, his claim to being the author of *The Disappointment* is tenuous in the extreme.

Leacock is tentatively suggested as the comedy's possible author by O. G. T. Sonneck, for many years the music librarian of the Library of Congress and a tireless and brilliant commentator on American music. In his *Early Opera in America* (1915) and elsewhere, Sonneck states that the authorship of *The Disappointment* is in sufficiently serious question to force it to be listed as "Barton" in the Library. Furthermore, Sonneck suggests that Leacock has some claim on the authorship, a suggestion based on certain structural and stylistic similarities that he has noted in *The Disappointment* and *The Fall of British Tyranny*.

Unfortunately, Sonneck does not amplify his suggestion, and I am forced to observe that a careful reading of both plays has revealed few similarities other than that both plays were written in the same part of the world, in the same century, and in a common language. The two plays seem almost totally different in style, language, theme, characterization, and intent—so different, in fact, that it seems an empty exercise to compare them.

This, then, is the bulk of the evidence to support John Leacock's nomination as the author of *The Disappointment*. It is far from conclusive, but more than that it is based upon a simple error on Dunlap's part and an unlikely and highly subjective comparison by Sonneck.[11]

The evidence for Thomas Forrest is no greater in quantity, it must be admitted, but taken in the aggregate it is more convincing. To begin with, Forrest is given as the author of the piece by John Fanning Watson, editor of the *Annals of Philadelphia and Pennsylvania*, a prime source of information concerning Philadelphia in the colonial period. Compiled in 1823, Watson's *Annals* is amazingly accurate and is taken at face value by numerous local historians. In this work Watson relates the story of Forrest's original practical joke, gives us the matter of Armbruster's involvement, and tells of the resulting play. Written before Dunlap's history, Watson's *Annals* may be taken as more factual (at least in this instance) and in fact has been considered so by Philadelphia historians—Forrest's authorship of the work has rarely been questioned by these local experts.

Furthermore, Thomas Forrest is listed as the author in several copies of *The Disappointment* held by the Library Company of Philadelphia and the Library of Congress. In a number of these copies the phrase "written by Colonel Thomas Forrest of Germantown," or some variant of this, appears handwritten on the flyleaves. While by no means conclusive, these addenda lend credence to the proposition that Forrest was in fact the author of the play.

With the exception of Sonneck no modern historian seriously doubts Forrest's authorship. Charles Durang concurs in *The Philadelphia Stage . . . 1749 to 1855*, as does Thomas Pollock in *The Philadelphia Theatre in the Eighteenth Century*, the two standard works on the subject. Hugh S. Rankin's *The Theatre in Colonial America* states categorically that "Andrew Barton" was "a pseudonym adopted by . . . Thomas Forrest of Germantown." These are but three examples to illustrate my contention that if Forrest was not the author of *The Disappointment*, no conclusive evidence has come to light to advance another claimant. The weight of circumstance and tradition heavily favors Forrest's claim to the authorship.

It would serve no real purpose to describe in great detail the life and career of Thomas Forrest, as neither was of a theatrical or literary nature and thus would be outside the scope of this study. *The Disappointment* is his only known work, and its cancellation seems to have stifled the creative urge in the young man. We know that he was born in 1747 in Philadelphia, the son of William Forrest and Sarah Hall.

He attended David James Dove's school in Vidal's Alley, where he came to know John Reily, the model for Parchment in the play.

Forrest's public career began with the Revolution when, at twenty-nine, he was appointed a captain of a company of marines in 1776, and served with Arnold's floating battery on the Delaware. Where or in what manner Forrest acquired the requisite knowledge of artillery is unknown—perhaps he was self-taught, as was Henry Knox, Washington's artillery expert. At any rate, Forrest was commissioned a captain in General Thomas Proctor's Pennsylvania Artillery in October of 1776, and served in that unit until 1781, when he resigned as a colonel. During the Revolution he served gallantly and well, distinguishing himself at the Battle of Trenton in an artillery duel with Hessian batteries on High Street. He was wounded at the Brandywine, and took part in the battle for what was to become his home, Germantown. In the latter instance he was court-martialed after the engagement for "neglect of Duty and with disobedience of Orders to the prejudice of the Service," and found guilty on both counts. The offense could not have been as grievous as the charges imply, as Forrest was only reprimanded in General Orders, a mild sentence.

After the war he established himself as a stockbroker in Philadelphia, a profession at which he must have prospered, for he bought a prominent country estate in Germantown in 1792. He served several terms as a member of the Pennsylvania Assembly and as a representative to the sixteenth and seventeenth Congresses. He died at his home in Germantown on Sunday, March 20, 1825, at the age of 78.

Little is known of Forrest's character, although he did have a reputation as a wit and practical joker when young. An inference about his impetuosity may be made from an incident during the Battle of Trenton, when Washington found it necessary to command him to lay his guns properly before firing them, and from his court-martial after Germantown. Modern historians have suggested that he was involved in "The Great Balloon Hoax" of 1783, but nothing other than his reputation for practical jokes is given as a basis for judgment. He must have been an emotional man, since, when reintroduced to Lafayette after the war, "he fell on his neck and wept like a child." Aside from these scraps, however, there are no further hints or clues to his character.[12]

Conjecture will never take the place of solid fact, but in the absence of such evidence, informed conjecture is the most reliable aid we possess. Perhaps the controversy over the authorship of *The Disappoint-*

ment will never be resolved; at best the question must remain open until new evidence is uncovered. Despite all this, I believe that there is sufficient reason to offer Thomas Forrest as the author of *The Disappointment*.

The Play

To a great extent, *The Disappointment* was influenced both directly and indirectly by *The Beggar's Opera*, John Gay's highly popular ballad opera of 1728. A smash hit from its opening, *The Beggar's Opera* soon became part of the production repertoire of virtually every English acting company. It was first produced in this country by the Murray-Kean Company in New York in 1750, and remained one of the staples of that short-lived group. The Hallam Company, which would be merged with Douglass and his actors to form the London Company of Comedians, performed the work for the first time in Philadelphia in 1759, during their first visit to that city. Forrest would have been only twelve years old, but it is certainly within the realm of conjecture that he might have seen that performance. If he had not been taken to the theater in Society Hill by his Quaker parents, it is possible that he was familiar with the play in print. *The Beggar's Opera* was sufficiently popular to warrant publication on several occasions.[13]

A major claim to fame for *The Beggar's Opera* is that it was the first of the "ballad operas," a form developed in England that was very popular in its time but did not survive the eighteenth century. The two most important features of the ballad opera are its use of dramatically integrated lyrics set to traditional or popular songs, and an infusion of social and political satire, particularly in the introduction of *roman à clef* characters. *The Beggar's Opera* and its hero, the highwayman Macheath, were seen by many as a satiric portrait of Robert Walpole, then prime minister. Walpole himself may have seen the resemblance, for he attempted to block publication of the work and of its sequel, *Polly*.

The first of these characteristics is quite evident in *The Disappointment*. The play contains eighteen airs, or ballads, with new lyrics pertinent to the plot or character written for them. Two of these airs, "Over the Hills and Far Away" and "The Lass of Patie's Mill," were used by Gay, and constitute the most direct proof that Forrest knew of and was influenced by the earlier play. Too, there seems to be some small *hommage* to Gay in Forrest's naming his heroine Lucy, possibly in imitation of Lucy Lockit—although the two characters are quite different, aside from their both being in love.

The second feature of ballad opera, a satiric plot and characters, is well represented in *The Disappointment*. As the history of the aborted production illustrates, the characters in the play had their counterparts in real life, and these characters were so closely drawn to life that the real butts of the original joke found the representation of their embarrassment on the stage unsupportable.

From these features—the popularity of *The Beggar's Opera* in this country at the time, the inclusion of two songs from the original work in *The Disappointment*, and the creation of characters with actual social counterparts—it seems obvious that Gay's work had perhaps the most direct influence on Forrest and his play.

Another strong influence on Forrest was the then-new and increasingly popular form of drama known as sentimental comedy. This form of comedy began as a reaction to the cynical heartlessness of the Restoration playwrights and developed into a style of drama that emphasized natural goodness in its characters as a virtue preferable to sophistication, and emphasized the belief that the function of comedy was to correct vice through the evocation of laughter. To the sentimentalists, comedy existed to correct deformity of character through the triumph of virtue and by holding vice up to ridicule and eventual reformation. Along with these high goals, sentimental comedy would also carry out the function of ridding the theater of those indecencies that its advocates felt had blackened the world of the Restoration. Leonard Welsted summed up the purpose and plan of sentimental comedy in a prologue to one of the most popular and influential examples of the form, Sir Richard Steele's *The Conscious Lovers*: " 'Tis yours with breeding to refine the age. / To chasten wit, and moralize the stage." This function of sentimental comedy was the one that most appealed to the American audiences of the period. Theater-going stood no chance of being accepted as part of the American scene if it were done in the name of pure amusement. This was considered self-indulgent at best and perniciously idle at worst, particularly in Quaker Philadelphia, where idleness was feared more than epidemic. Going to the theater, if such an activity were to be tolerated, must have some purpose other than amusement—it must in some way elevate or instruct the moral faculties of the viewers. Douglass, for his part, seemed well aware of this feeling on the part of the communities in which he played, for he passed up no chance to point out the high moral tone of his presentations.

Forrest seemed well aware of this requirement, too, for in both the preface and prologue to *The Disappointment* he is at some pains to draw, describe, and emphasize the moral precepts inherent in the work. While he briefly suggests that one of the purposes he had in writing the play was "the necessity of adding to the entertainment of the city," he dwells at length upon the moral of the work, "that mankind ought to be contented with their respective stations, to follow their vocations with honesty and industry—the only sure way to riches."

Furthermore, Forrest is unabashedly moralistic in the prologue. Presuming he wrote it—not always the case in this period—the prologue to *The Disappointment* is almost overwhelming in its insistence that the sole purpose for the existence of the play is to draw several moral precepts to the attention of the audience. To begin with, the prologist is of the opinion that the business of the theater is "to point out vice in its deformity; / Make virtue fair shine eminently bright, / Rapture the breast and captivate the sight." Once this high function is given to the theater, the inevitable comparison is drawn between the church and the playhouse: "No matter which, the pulpit or the stage, / Condemn the vice and folly of the age."

Superficially, it would seem that the moralistic principles of sentimental comedy have been well served by Forrest. While it is apparent that the author's intent should be taken at face value, there are certain lapses from the tradition of sentimental comedy in *The Disappointment* that suggest the moralistic tone of the play is in large measure feigned—none too skillfully tacked onto the work in an effort to satisfy the prevalent attitudes of the potential viewers.

First, there is the matter of ribald humor. While this element, most apparent in the scenes with Moll Placket, gives freshness and vitality to the play for the modern reader, it was condemned by the few nineteenth-century critics. Seilhamer does not equivocate on this point: "A much graver objection to the comedy, and one that should have prevented its acceptance in the first instance, was its coarseness and immorality, making it unfit for the stage."[14] The widely held opinion that Douglass was fortunate in presenting *The Prince of Parthia* in place of *The Disappointment* is in large measure based upon the lack of indecency and robustness in the tragedy. Moll Placket and her shaky *menage à trois* belong more properly in a Restoration comedy or French farce than in the stifling moral atmosphere of Sir Richard Steele or George Colman.

There is a vitality and naturalness in the scenes condemned as "low" or "obscene" that is entirely missing in the more traditional, sentimental

ones, and this loss gives the latter an air of artificiality that is unmistakable. Compare, for instance, the robust reality of Topinlift's statements of affection and healthy lust in II, i to the formal apostrophes of
Meanwell and Lucy in I, vi. The latter example seems foreign and
formal for a twenty-year-old writer, while the former seems much more
in keeping with the light-hearted character of Forrest.

Second, Forrest violates a strong element of the sentimental tradition, the display of parental authority and youthful submission to it.
Meanwell and Lucy are forbidden to marry by her guardian and uncle,
Washball, on the grounds that when he acquires his share of the buried
treasure he expects to find, young Meanwell will be socially beneath his
niece. In II, iii Meanwell effectively seduces Lucy from her sense of
obligation to her uncle's wishes, and they elope. While the superiority
of a marriage based on love to one based on arrangement is a staple of
the sentimental tradition, it is nonetheless the case that such a blatant
example of youthful rebellion would violate the decorum that is an in-
tegral part of the sentimental character. Lucy's decision to ignore her
uncle's wishes and orders is based upon a strong affection for and physical attraction to Meanwell, and not upon a quasi-philosophic examina-
tion of the conflict between love and duty. In other words, one song and
she's his.

Lastly, it seems fair to say that the element of correction through
ridicule, a strong feature of sentimental comedy, is very weak in the
script. If it is a function of the theater "to point out vice in its deformity" and, by implication, to correct and reform it, *The Disappointment* fails completely. The targets of the practical joke in the play are
not vicious in any sense of the word; they are merely stupid and
credulous. The "humorists" who set up the joke do not feel that they
are going to such elaborate lengths for any corrective purpose, but
rather as part of a "diversion," as one of them puts it. The expository
I, i gives no reason for the joke that is being planned other than mere
amusement. Any corrective value it may possess is added in the last
scene of the play, in a number of very inappropriate speeches delivered
by the dupes.

Given these shortcomings in *The Disappointment* as an example of
sentimental comedy, I think we can fairly say that the moralistic and
sentimental aspects of the work were added after the fact, as it were,
and should be considered as little more than catering to what Forrest
(and perhaps Douglass) felt were the standards of public taste. There
can be no question that these artificialities mar the work as a whole, but

if one can disregard them, the remaining portions of the play are worth dramatic analysis and critical praise.

The plot of *The Disappointment* is simple, if not simplistic, based on the establishment and execution of one action, the delusion of several credulous men into discovering a buried "treasure." There are two embryonic subplots—the Raccoon-Placket-Topinlift triangle and the Meanwell-Lucy romance—but neither is sufficiently well developed to warrant the title of subplot, nor are they integrated sufficiently into the main plot for us to say the play has a compound action. It is for the most part what the modern commercial theater would call a one-joke show.

This is not necessarily a drawback; successful and significant plays without number have been based upon one action—*Oedipus Rex* and Gogol's *The Inspector-General*, for example. What is difficult about a simple plot is that it requires great skill on the part of the playwright to avoid repetition of expository information, to condense stage time to avoid tedium, and to avoid creating characters with such minuteness as to overwhelm their actions. In two of these respects Forrest is quite successful; in the first he fails totally.

In the first act of *The Disappointment* we are given the information necessary to understand the action three separate and distinct times: first by the humorists, then by the dupes, and lastly by one of the dupes to Placket. The main action of the play is simply not sufficiently complicated to warrant such repetition, nor is the audience rewarded with new insights or implications by each repetition to justify this approach. It is simply an error in judgment on the young playwright's part. It is not, however, a fatal error, for the major scene in the work—the digging up of the treasure—is sufficiently interesting and amusing to permit the audience either to forget the somewhat tedious exposition or to forgive the playwright for the slow buildup.

Forrest's use of time is quite good, despite the flaws just mentioned. Once the plan has been activated, we progress quite rapidly to the obligatory climax, when the hoax is revealed. A minor complication, Washball's duplicity in trying to take the treasure for himself, only adds to the comic tension before the revelation and is skillfully done. The digressions—for example, the low-comic Trushoop and Mrs. Trushoop scene—are held to minimum length and contain enough physical action to avoid becoming talky, while the bawdy humor of the Moll Placket scenes makes them sufficiently entertaining in their own right not to distract us from the main action. In all, the play moves quickly, with sufficiently entertaining digressions, from point of attack to climax. The denouement is tedious, but this is due in large measure to the moralizing speeches of Raccoon and Washball in particular.

The Disappointment is imperfect in its plotting, but for the most part it goes well. The main action is sufficiently strong to keep our interest, and the attempted subplots are either amusing in themselves or mercifully brief. A flaw in Forrest's plotting lies in his inability to handle the traditional complications. In the traditional simple plot, the protagonist desires to put a plan into action, against opposition, and either succeeds or alters his purpose. In *The Disappointment* the plan (the buried-treasure joke) is not opposed by anyone—indeed it succeeds spectacularly—and the element of dramatic suspense ("Will it work—won't it work?") is almost entirely missing. Forrest seems to have been aware of this defect, as he introduces the possibility that the king's collector might confiscate the "treasure," but this complication comes too late in the play to be of any dramatic value. Had Forrest established Washball's treachery of calling in the authorities earlier in the action, the play would have been substantially improved. Consequently, the only suspense in the work lies in waiting for the discovery of the joke and the reactions of the dupes to it. This may readily be seen as a thin thread upon which to hang a comedy and Forrest seems to have known it, for he takes some pains to make the play short and filled with incident, mostly quite independent of the main action.

The characters are broadly drawn, befitting a shallow farce. The conspirators, Hum, Parchment, Quadrant, and Rattletrap, are virtually indistinguishable one from the other. Were we not given some individual touches of characterization dialogue, particularly in the case of Parchment and Rattletrap, it would be impossible to tell the humorists apart. Although it seems certain that Forrest modeled some of his characters upon acquaintances then living in Philadelphia, we have no way of knowing how exact the portraits are, except in the case of Parchment. Parchment was modeled on John Reily, a spelling-master at the school Forrest attended. Reily was admired by his students, and would upon occasion amuse the young men by affecting a highly exaggerated manner of speaking, filled with high-sounding, sonorous legalisms. Parchment's long, funny speech in I, i, in which he denies any interest in violating the law, is thought to have been based upon the mimicry with which Reily would entertain his students.

For the most part the characters are quite bland and undeveloped. As suggested earlier, this is not necessarily a drawback for the sort of play Forrest was writing, as a farce cannot support characters of any complexity. It is enough to know that Rattletrap, for example, has a certain knowledge of astrology and necromancy—no further information about his character is necessary for us to appreciate and understand his function in the piece.

The dupes are characterized by their origins. Trushoop is Irish, and therefore expresses himself in a continual series of Irish bulls, or humorously self-contradictory statements ("Dis day will be a bad night for me."). He is given to loud arguments with his wife, for all the neighborhood to hear, and drinks to excess upon every occasion. In short, Trushoop is nothing more than one of a long line of "Irishmen" who have amused English and American audiences for centuries, and who bear little resemblance to their ethnic prototypes. Nonetheless, Trushoop performs an efficient function in the play, for all his stock-character staginess, because he is so amusing.

Much the same can be said for McSnip, the Scots tailor. He is a ferocious figure, much given to swinging his broadsword in fits of rage. He is not as well developed a stock character as Trushoop, displaying few of the traditional qualities of the stage Scotchman other than a short and violent temper. At one point in the play he suggests a large reward to someone, surely a violation of the theatrical "law" that all Scots are stingy.

Of the three ethnic characters of the play, surely Raccoon is the most interesting, for a number of reasons. First, there is some real question of Raccoon's origins; his name is not a label, as McSnip or Trushoop, and the dialogue given him is written in a remarkable fashion, resembling nothing more than the stage Negro of the nineteenth century. It is this dialogue that has led several critics to assert that Forrest would have been the first to portray an American Negro on the stage, if *The Disappointment* had been performed. This is an important matter, for the Negro, along with the Indian and the Yankee, is one of the "native characters" that have strongly influenced the later American theater.

There is much to recommend the position that Raccoon is intended by the author to be black. The accent as written, with its substitution of "d" for "t" and "th," "b" for "v" and so on, closely resembles the dialogue of numerous "coon" characters in the next century. Furthermore, at one point, in great excitement, Trushoop demands that Raccoon shut his "black mout'," and at another, when Raccoon suggests that he has courage enough to face the devils surrounding the treasure, Hum responds by saying, "You're a lucky man—your courage is constitutional." This may be taken as a reference to Raccoon's dark skin, and its inability to grow pale with fear. These and other considerations have led the finest of the modern historians of the colonial theater to the conclusion that "with the character 'Raccoon,' Forrest introduced the first Negro character in American drama and his was the first attempt to adapt Negro dialect to the stage."[15]

There are some other facts that may contradict this conclusion, however. It is difficult to accept the idea of a black man cohabiting with a white woman on the stage in eighteenth-century Philadelphia, or a black man being a member of a Masonic lodge with a white membership. Raccoon does both; he keeps Placket in concubinage, and he makes much of his Masonic relationships and position. Furthermore, Raccoon is a member of the militia and prides himself on his knowledge of military matters. There were no Negro members of the militia in Philadelphia at that time, although several black men served in the Revolution in later years—one, interestingly, in Forrest's own outfit.

The name "Raccoon" should not be given the ethnic connotation in this situation that it would possess in the late nineteenth century, that is, as a derogatory synonym for a black man. In the period of *The Disappointment*, "raccoon" was a nickname given to members of the militia, especially of the New Jersey militia. This, coupled with the character Raccoon's professed expertise in things military, leads me to believe that Forrest picked the name for its military rather than ethnic connotations. Furthermore, at the time the play was written there was, on the eastern bank of the Delaware River, a small town called Raccoon, populated almost entirely by Swedish immigrants. In view of this, it is my opinion that Forrest might be attempting to portray a Swede in the character of Raccoon.[16] It is an historical fact that there were many more Swedish immigrants in and around Philadelphia at that time than Negroes, and the type would not only be more recognizable to Philadelphia audiences, but more acceptable as well.

The immediate objection to this supposition concerns the stage-Negro dialect that Forrest has written so well. In answer, let me suggest that the dialogue is written *too* well in the case of Raccoon, not having the inconsistencies and errors of orthography that pepper the lines given to McSnip and Trushoop. It is difficult to accept the idea that while Forrest wrote inaccurate and inconsistent "Irish" and "Scots" he wrote perfect "Negro." It seems much easier to accept the idea that Forrest, in writing Raccoon's lines, was attempting to write down the particular pronunciation of the Swedish, a most difficult task when one considers that a salient characteristic of Scandinavian speech is its rhythmic flow, and not a certain, consistently characterizing pronunciation.

Seilhamer has suggested that Raccoon is supposed to be German, presumably modeled on Armbruster, but certain statements Raccoon makes in II, i make this suggestion untenable. He tells Placket that he is unable to read the German almanac she presents to him, which hardly suggests a Teutonic origin.[17]

While it is of course impossible to determine exactly what Forrest had in mind in writing Raccoon's peculiar dialect, we can say with some certainty that he intended the character to be a figure of fun, one recognizable to the audience, and a member of a minority. This is undoubtedly his intention with the other ethnic characters in the play, and it seems reasonable that he would choose for his subjects minority figures well known in Philadelphia at the time. While there were Negroes, both slave and free, in the city, their numbers were small compared to other ethnic groups, among them the Swedish. I think it not unreasonable to assume that Forrest chose three groups which the audience could both identify with and be amused by.

It is with personal reluctance that I propose Raccoon to be of Swedish rather than Negro origin. Had he been intended by the author to be black, it would represent a major literary accomplishment. Until further evidence appears, however, Rankin's statement must remain conjecture rather than fact.

The other characters in *The Disappointment* are of no particular interest and function mainly as operatives in the progression of the plot. Washball the barber is a reasonably well-drawn fussy, frightened old man, not without a touch of androgyny; but the others are wooden and without definition. Still, farce cannot support complex characters, nor is the proper emphasis in this form on characterization; the characters are slaves to the plot and work to do its will. Forrest seems to have recognized this, and sketched his people with broad, shallow strokes.

Forrest's dialogue is satisfactory, but uneven in quality. The vocal patterns of the play are generally good, which is to say that the dialogue is easy to read from an actor's point of view. There are exceptions, to be sure—several of the sentences are too long and contain too many dependent clauses that tend to obscure the meaning when spoken aloud —but in the main the dialogue is theatrically effective.

In matching characters and their language, Forrest is inconsistent. Quadrant, for example, employs no metaphoric or descriptive language to help us understand his character, as opposed to Topinlift, who is given maritime terminology to delineate and color his. With the exception of the harangue already commented upon, Parchment engages in no further legalisms, while the general tone of the language spoken by Washball does give the impression of a rather fussy hairdresser. The dialect characters show much the same inconsistency; at times Trushoop sounds Scotch, and McSnip uses Irishisms almost as often.

There are few verbal digressions for their own sake and little extraneous dialogue. Exceptions to this, of course, are the moralizing speeches of Washball and Raccoon in the last scene; but when these are compared to the sententious homilies of many of Forrest's dramatic contemporaries, they are not objectionable.

There are few lines in the play that are funny for their own sake. The humor of the piece lies in situation rather than in funny remarks. Of the infrequent verbal jokes the majority are Raccoon's—for example, when searching for protection in prayer, he begins to recite Masonic ritual; but these are few and far between. In all, the dialogue is utilitarian and, like the characterizations, subservient to the plot.

The theme of *The Disappointment* is stated baldly by the author, in both the preface and the body of the work. It seems to be Forrest's purpose to show the debilitating effects of credulity and cupidity and, at the beginning and end of the play, he is at some pains to point this out with great and perhaps excessive clarity. This moral theme is stated too clearly to be taken seriously, however, and it is my opinion that Forrest's "message" is something other than a farcical restatement of the Pardoner's text, *radix malorum est cupiditas*. In making this the ostensible theme of the work Forrest is doing nothing more than satisfying the dramatic fashion of the time, which was to sentimentalize both human and theatrical activities in order to emphasize the redeemability of man. I hardly think the practical joke from which the play developed had the correction of the benighted as its motive. It simply does not seem consistent with our knowledge of Forrest and his friends to believe that they indulged in the joke for the sake of social improvement. It seems safe to suppose that the joke was pulled for its own sake. This is not to imply that Forrest was hypocritical in either the preface or the play; it is simply to say that the sentimental theme of the play is applied to rather than adduced from the inspirational event.

The philosophic basis for *The Disappointment* lies in the traditional conflict between "crabbed age and youth." "See, how to fool the old folk, the young folk put their heads together," says Grumio in *The*

Taming of the Shrew, and this observation seems to be at the bottom of the action of the play. Forrest and his friends saw, in the credulity of many concerning the possibility of locally buried treasure, a classic opportunity to demonstrate the intellectual superiority of the young, and availed themselves of the chance. The young making fools of the old has been a staple of the comic theater at least since *The Clouds* of Aristophanes: I suggest that this awareness was not only at the heart of the original joke but also suggested to Forrest the dramatic mode as the proper vehicle for its preservation.

The Disappointment is described as a comic opera, undoubtedly to increase interest in the play, as the term was then quite new, at least to English and American audiences. While *opéras comiques* can be said to have originated in France in the earlier part of the century under René LeSage, and in definition closely resembled *The Disappointment*, it is certain that Forrest drew his inspiration not from the French but from the English theater. In the latter instance, comic opera was the successor to ballad opera, typified by Gay's *Beggar's Opera*. The leading proponent of comic opera was Isaac Bickerstaff, whose *Maid of the Mill*, for example, did much to establish the popularity of this new form. Comic opera was characterized by sentimental plots and original music; ballad opera, as described elsewhere, depended upon satiric plotting and new lyrics set to traditional or popular tunes.[18]

Musically, *The Disappointment* is a hybrid, containing elements of both ballad and comic opera, as these forms were defined in the eighteenth century. The plot is satiric, although it contains sentimental morals and attitudes, and the music is derivative in origin, with newly constructed lyrics.

Forrest is inconsistent in the originality he brought to bear on the new lyrics incorporated into the play. In several cases (e.g., "Nancy Dawson" and "Kitty the Nonpareil") he did nothing more than alter the names in the original songs to those of the appropriate characters in his play, while in others ("Over the Hills and Far Away" and "The Lass of Patie's Mill") he significantly alters the lyrics to suit the dramatic requirements of the moment. Generally, however, his use of incorporated music is not consistently skillful. In the majority of cases the songs do not emanate naturally from the action or the characters. Instead, they are somewhat roughly interpolated, and often are introduced with such artificial lead-ins as Rattletrap's "There's nothing like putting a good face on these matters—if you'll all bear a chorus, I'll sing you a song before we set off." Occasionally the songs are well integrated and show some technical skill on Forrest's part, as in II, iii, when Lucy's decision to elope is made in song, and Meanwell's request for haste is expressed in the refrain; but for the most part the songs intrude into the action, rather than grow from it. In fact, it seems not unreasonable to say that the *The Disappointment* would be a better play if most of the songs were deleted.

The visual aspects of the play are not remarkable. Forrest does show some theatrical awareness in II, ii, the climactic scene in terms of spectacle, when he requires several special effects such as fireworks, offstage noises, and the "ghost of Blackbeard" which appears and must "spit fire"; but in the main *The Disappointment* contains little else that would delight the eye, nor does it require stage effects that would tax the imagination or equipment of potential producers. The work could have been quite easily staged by the American Company, both technically and artistically. Indeed, the most difficult technical requirements in the play would be the fireballs in II, ii, and these could be created by the time-honored method of throwing on stage wads of cotton soaked in sulphur and brine solution and set on fire. Chemicals could be added to the solution to color the fire, and quite spectacular effects achieved.

The Disappointment would have been quite easy to produce in its acting requirements as well. We know a good deal about the members of Douglass's troupe, and given the eighteenth-century practice of "lines of business"—a system wherein certain types of characters were played consistently by certain members of the company—we could state with some assurance that the company did have an actor or actress who could easily have created each of the characters. It is not germane to this study to establish a probable casting; those interested in such speculation may look to Seilhamer's tentative suggestions as to who would have played whom.[19]

In summary, then, *The Disappointment* is the work of a gifted amateur with some theatrical talent and imagination. The work lies well within the eighteenth-century traditional mode of sentimental comedy with some interesting lapses, many of them deliberate, from the current fashion. The interpolation of songs into the structure is artificial, as are the homiletics at the conclusion, but these practices are without doubt the result of the dramatic pressures of the period and represent not so much a structural fault in form as a deliberate catering to prevailing tastes. This pandering may be felt by some to be the work of a literary toady; I prefer to consider it the result of Forrest's awareness that the public's values must be respected if a piece of dramatic art is to succeed

at all. The eighteenth-century English theater recognized, in the words
of one of its own, that "the drama's laws the drama's patrons give; / For
we who live to please, must please to live."

There is a breezy innocence about *The Disappointment* that covers
a multitude of flaws. The joke played on the dupes is not harmful, save
to their vanity, nor are the perpetrators in any way vicious. The play
is not bitter, nor is it cynical; rather, it is youthfully naïve in a particularly engaging manner. In this it seems to reflect, metaphorically, the
attitude and character of the new nation for which the author would
soon be called upon to give so much. Forrest seemed to be aware of
many of the requirements an American audience would soon impose
upon the drama offered it. He understood, or perhaps experienced un-
consciously, many of the elements that would in time constitute a unique
manner of viewing the drama, a manner that we can only call American.

The American audience was—and is—almost aggressively unso-
phisticated; it is neither willing nor capable of following complex or
prolix arguments on the stage. It wants and will have action, spectacle,
and variety as well as simplicity. All of these, in varying degrees, *The
Disappointment* provides. Further, the American audience requires that
its plays have a justification for their existence; in other words, there
must be some reason for attending the theater other than for amusement's sake. Most often this requirement has resulted in American
drama's becoming almost militantly affirmative—a feeling well represented in the positive moral atmosphere of *The Disappointment*.

Furthermore, the American audience has always shown a preference
for comedy. Forrest realized this to a degree his contemporary Thomas
Godfrey never did. Certainly part of the failure of *The Prince of Parthia*
lay in the fact that it was a tragedy, and the American grain, in its
theatrical preferences at least, is deeply comic. We seem to prefer our
comedy to be mildly satiric, and most often satiric of ourselves and our
institutions if the satire does not bite or corrode. Perhaps it is closer
to the point to say that American audiences have been ever ready to
laugh at their own foibles and fads, as witness Tyler's *The Contrast*,
Mowatt's *Fashion*, Mitchell's *The New York Idea*, and our contemporary Neil Simon, to name a few. Each of these playwrights has seized
upon a social whim and satirized it for the delight of those who did not
or would not share in the absurdity presented to them. Forrest places
himself quite in this vein and, historically, at its head.

Americans also have had a fondness for the musical theater. Although it is certain that Forrest was catering to the current theatrical

fad of comic opera, it is not improbable that he recognized this develop-
ing aspect of the American audience, if only subconsciously, and incorporated it in *The Disappointment.*

As a nation of immigrants, Americans have been ready to laugh at
the ethnic minorities to which we all at least originally belonged. The
tradition of ethnic humor is deep in the American theater and drama,
and it may be said that this tradition began with Forrest.

It is perhaps historically untrue that the popular American theater
began with Forrest and his abortive play, but many elements of that
form are apparent in the work, and the author deserves credit for his
apparent awareness of these elements. The virtues of the piece are
humble, to be sure, but taken in the balance, they outweigh the faults
sufficiently to make *The Disappointment* a play that deserves a wider
audience.

The Theater

The Southwark Theater was the second playhouse built in that then-
suburban area near Philadelphia. Seven years earlier, in 1759, Douglass
had built a theater on Society Hill, which his company had used for
only one season. Little is known of this older theater except the fact
that "Douglass purchased a complete stock of new scenery" for its
opening. Authorities seem in agreement that the Society Hill theater
was little more than a temporary building, particularly as there is no
record of its being used after 1759.

Douglass and the American Company of Comedians made their
second visit to Philadelphia in 1766. Upon learning that the company
planned to return to the city, religious conservatives began to rail
against theater in general and actors in particular, both from the pulpit
and the press. Petitions were offered to the governor to restrain the
actors from performance, a move that had proved partially successful
in the past. This time, however, the petitions failed, and the "unco' guid"
watched in pious rage as a new Temple of Satan was raised in Southwark.

The new playhouse gave the impression that theater had returned
to Philadelphia to stay. Although what we know of the structure leads
us to believe that it was, by modern standards, inadequate in virtually
every respect, there was at the time an unmistakable air of permanence
about the building, built of brick and costing twice as much as the older
Society Hill playhouse. This impression of permanence was well founded,

as the Southwark Theater continued to be used in one capacity or another until its destruction by fire in 1912.[20]

A visitor to the Southwark, writing some twenty years after its construction, has left us with the only description that is in any way contemporary. It is not complimentary. "The building," he wrote, "compared with the new houses, was an ugly, ill-contrived affair outside and inside. The stage lighted by plain oil lamps without glasses. The view from the boxes was intercepted by large square wooden pillars supporting the upper tier and roof. It was contended by many, at the time, that the front bench in the gallery was the best seat for a fair view of the whole stage." The exterior was painted a dull red, the foundations in brick and the upper story in wood. A drawing of the Southwark shows us a plain structure, unprepossessing in every way, with little more to distinguish it from a warehouse than a strange cupola atop the pitched roof and three windows on the second floor facing the street. Despite this outward appearance, it is important to remember that the Southwark was the largest and best-equipped theater of its time in North America. The entire building was ninety-five feet long by fifty feet wide, and would seat approximately 400 spectators. The construction cost (some 600 pounds) did not include the new scenery that Douglass had traveled to England to obtain earlier that year—scenery executed by Nicholas Thomas Doll, "principal scene painter" to the Theatre Royal, Covent Garden. Despite the fact that the Southwark was imperfect and rather quickly became obsolete, at the time of its construction it had no equal in North America and compared favorably with a number of small theaters in England in capacity, comfort, and theatrical capability.[21]

Although no plan of the theater exists, the auditorium was undoubtedly arranged in the traditional English pattern: box, pit, and gallery. Douglass probably had a master plan for the various theaters he built in the colonies, and there is every reason to believe that the Chapel Street theater, the Southwark, and the John Street theater resembled one another as much as possible. Insofar as we have reasonably complete descriptions of the Chapel Street and John Street theaters, it can be assumed that many if not all of their features were incorporated in the Philadelphia playhouse.

By virtue of this reasoning, we can state with some definition that the Southwark had a sloping pit, at least one tier of side boxes, boxes on the stage itself, and a gallery above the boxes, facing the proscenium and flanking the pit. The pit was entered through an underground passage, "not well-lighted, . . . which opened by a door on one side, the left; the other was the west wall of the passage." Side aisles in the pit itself gave access to the low, backless benches that filled the area.

The boxes, small individual compartments in the first tier above the pit, were entered through a narrow staircase that, in the case of the Chapel Street theater, "rose from a small lobby, containing a paybooth, near the front of the theater." The arrangement at the Southwark must have been similar. In an attempt to resemble the more elaborate English theaters, the boxes were decorated with red wallpaper, in imitation of the red moreen hangings traditional in the Theatre Royal, Covent Garden. The fronts of the boxes, as well as the entire interior of the theater, were painted an unattractive shade of green that again was traditional.

Above the boxes was the gallery, an open seating area containing the cheapest seats and thereby attracting the poorer and less-well-behaved patrons. These customers believed, with some justification, that they could control the performances they attended to a degree that would strike the modern theatergoer as intolerable, through their tendency to show verbal and physical approval or disapproval of the events on stage. For this reason tl.e patrons of the gallery were called, and called themselves, the "Gallery Gods."[22]

Lighting the auditorium was a constant problem for the eighteenth-century theater manager, and the problems in lighting the Southwark were typical of the period. The crucial problem was economic; the cheapest candles, made of beef tallow, cost a penny per pound, and for one performance of *Othello* in the Chapel Street theater in 1762 Douglass was forced to use fourteen pounds of tallow candles, no small expense for the time. There were two objections to tallow candles: they dripped terribly, staining the clothes of those unfortunate enough to sit beneath them, and they smelled horribly. Nonetheless, the economics of theatrical production dictated their widespread use.

The alternatives to tallow candles were oil lamps or the ruinously expensive spermaceti candles. All three of these light sources were doubtless employed at the Southwark; the oil lamps, dishes of whale oil with floating, smoky wicks, were reserved for the pit passages and the gallery, while a combination of tallow and spermaceti candles were placed in sconces or "branches" on the box fronts and with the boxes themselves. It is quite likely that the oil lamps in the gallery were extinguished before the performance began, as were the spermaceti candles, while the tallow candles were permitted to burn down to the holders during the course of the evening's entertainment, lending some slight il-

lumination to the stage. It is not known if any of the Douglass theaters—
the Chapel Street, the Southwark, or the John Street—had chandeliers
in the auditorium, but if Douglass did everything in his power to recreate
the theaters he had known in England, we may assume that they did.[23]

The boxes and the gallery formed a U-shape facing the stage and
proscenium arch. A portion of the stage extended into the auditorium,
beyond the proscenium arch with its green curtain. This apron, as it
was called, was the main acting area, the actors rarely venturing upstage
beyond the arch. The apron was entered through two doors at either
side of the proscenium arch, a practice in the English theater since the
Restoration. Above each of these doors were boxes, the most expensive
seats in the theater, and ones that provided a good view of the patrons
occupying them, if not of the stage. The apron and stage were raised
approximately five feet above the level of the pit, and separated from it
by a low wooden paling, topped by iron spikes.

Nothing is known of the dimensions of the proscenium arch, or of
its decoration. It was the fashion in the eighteenth century to decorate
the proscenium as elaborately as possible, in contrast to the present practice, and we may conclude that Douglass followed this custom in the
Southwark insofar as he was financially able. An earlier theater in Philadelphia, a temporary structure in Plumsted's warehouse, had the proscenium arch "inscribed (with) the words *Totus Mundus agit His-
trionem* in imitation of the motto above the stage at Drury Lane"; so it
is probable that Douglass decorated the proscenium in the far more
elaborate Southwark, but to what extent is unknown.

As mentioned earlier, the main curtain of the Southwark was green,
similar to the one used at the John Street. It was raised to begin the play
and remained raised throughout the performance, not lowered for act
breaks or scene shifts as it is today. Any changing of the scenery was
done in full view of the audience by a complicated arrangement of sliding panels and drop pieces and indeed, if the shifts were done professionally and smoothly, provided no small part of the evening's entertainment.[24]

The scenery used in the Southwark was probably of the type known
as "wing and shutter." This term described a method of arranging flat
pieces of scenery parallel to the proscenium arch, each piece or "wing"
with a portion of the scene painted on it. At the back wall of the stage,
or near it, two large wings would project onto the stage until they met,
forming a solid scene hiding the upstage area. These pieces were, of
course, the "shutters."

The flats, both wings and shutters, would be painted in perspective to represent a certain place. Other places could be painted on other flats which were placed directly behind the wings and shutters. When the scene was to change, the wing pieces and shutters nearest the audience would slide horizontally offstage, revealing the new scene behind them. Thus, in *The Disappointment* the first scene, a tavern, would slide away after the exit of the characters, revealing the second scene, the street before Trushoop's house, behind it. To return to the tavern scene, as is required in Act I, scene vii, was a simple matter with this scenic arrangement: the first set of wings and shutters would be pushed back into their onstage position, thus hiding the scenery behind them.

The area above the wings and shutters was undoubtedly concealed by borders—pieces of cloth suspended from a wooden framework, or gridiron, near the top of the theater. These borders could be painted to represent the sky, clouds, or leaves for exterior scenes and ceilings for interiors. Usually the borders were not shifted every time the wings and shutters were; a sky border could remain for all exteriors, for example, and a ceiling representation would serve for all interiors.

The advantages of wing-and-shutter scenery were manifold for a small provincial theater such as the Southwark. In the first place, this system eliminated the need for a cumbersome, complex, and expensive fly system, in which the scenery pieces were lifted to the top of the stagehouse by a series of pulleys, lines, and pinrails that in structure and operation much resembled the rigging of a sailing ship of the period. "Flown" scenery would become the standard shifting method in the next century, and indeed was not unknown in the eighteenth, particularly in the large English theater; but it seems beyond question that the Southwark employed the older, simpler system described. Another advantage of the sliding system was financial; it was much less expensive than the alternative.

Both the wings and shutters were held in position by grooves, created by strips of wood placed parallel to one another on either side of the piece to be shifted, and then nailed to the stage floor. The tops of the wings were held in place by a similar arrangement, a grooved piece of wood suspended from the gridiron. The modern sliding doors closely resemble this arrangement, although the scene pieces did not have wheels in tracks, commonly seen today.

There are no contemporary descriptions of the scene paintings at the Southwark; what we know of them we can only surmise from scanty references to the stock scenery at other theaters used by Douglass and the American Company, and from descriptions of scenery used in similar provincial theaters at the time.

Contrary to the present practice, the eighteenth-century theaters did not build and paint scenery for each production. The frequency of performances in the repertory system then employed, as well as the expense, precluded the creation of new sets for each play produced by any group. More important than the financial difficulties involved was the attitude of the audiences of the time toward scenery and scenic practices. To the theatergoer of this period, scenery provided nothing more than a broadly generalized backdrop to frame the actors and their actions. The emphasis was placed upon the play and the actors, not upon the environment produced by the scene painters. Some have said that the theatergoers were more concerned with the transcendent values of the plays they attended, rather than with the reality of the situation in which they took place. I think it is more accurate to say that the audiences that might have viewed *The Disappointment* were simply not realistically oriented, at least not where the theater was concerned. It mattered not to them that the garden exterior that had backed up last week's performance of *As You Like It* would serve this week as Lear's heath, or that the interior that represented Bonniface's tavern in *The Beaux' Stratagem* might bear an unmistakable similarity to the Tun Tavern, if it had been represented as planned in I, i and I, vii of Forrest's play. It was what happened in front of that scenery that interested them, not technical or visual verisimilitude.

For these and other reasons, it was the common procedure in the eighteenth century to provide each theater with a set of scenes, each representing a general locale, the less particularized the better. Douglass, as we know, had recently acquired a new set of scenes from England, painted by the English theater's foremost scenic artist. The cost of these pieces is unknown, but an earlier set of scenes painted for the theater on Society Hill had cost a hundred pounds, a very high price for such a set. It is more than likely that the new scenery for the Southwark cost much more, imported as it was, and created by Mr. Doll of the Theatre Royal, Covent Garden.

It seems likely that the scenery set imported by Douglass included a Formal Exterior, consisting perhaps of wings painted as hedges and topiary with a shutter set that represented a formal, landscaped vista with a cupola gazebo at the vanishing point. Complementing this would be the Rustic Exterior, with gnarled trees and rocks for the wings, and a back view of hills and mountains; a Fancy Interior and a Plain Interior; and a City Exterior, with the shutters and wings painted to represent buildings and streets. With these sets there were no doubt several sets of borders representing tree limbs and branches, sky and clouds, and formal and informal ceilings.

Each of these settings could be employed in *The Disappointment* and indeed would have fit most of the plays of the American Company's repertoire.[25] Although the settings used in the Southwark Theater may strike the modern reader as primitive, they did suffice under the somewhat peculiar scenic conventions of the time. With these stock settings the Southwark was capable, too, of an occasional "special effect." The Chapel Street theater used transparencies, a technique employing translucent linen stretched on frames across the stage which when lit from behind would become virtually transparent, and when lit from the front, almost opaque. Scenes could be painted with dyes on these pieces and, when the proper lighting was applied, would "appear" or "disappear" in a manner that delighted the amazed audiences. Although *The Disappointment* does not require transparencies, its successor *The Prince of Parthia* might—particularly in I, v, where "the Scene draws and discovers, in the inner Part of the Temple, a large Image of the Sun, with an altar before it." MacNamara feels that "the chances are excellent . . . that the 'Image of the Sun' was achieved by a transparent scene of some sort" (p. 67).

Another special effect that the Southwark was clearly capable of producing was the positioning of the shutters, or back scenes, at a point downstage of their usual position near the rear wall of the stagehouse. While this would have the effect of making the stage area more shallow, it would provide for another scene to be set up behind, or upstage of, the scene revealed to the audience. At the appropriate moment, the "scene would draw," in the phrase of the times, revealing the next scene upstage of it. That the Southwark was capable of these midstage shutter positions is evident from the stage direction in II, i of *The Disappointment*: "As they walk toward the upper part of the stage, a scene opens, and discovers a bed, table, and two bottles on it, with a broken glass over one of them and a candle stuck in the other."

This stage direction is interesting both because it demonstrates the capability of the Southwark to split the stage longitudinally and because it shows the emphasis placed on using properties and furniture to set the scene, lessening dependence upon specific scenery to create a sense of locale. The little touches of the bottles, candle, and broken glass provide a surprisingly realistic element to Moll Placket's tainted bedroom.[26]

Lighting the stage at the Southwark was as difficult as lighting the auditorium. Illumination of the actors, who, it will be remembered, used the apron or forestage almost exclusively, was achieved by footlights made of tin troughs with oil and wicks, perhaps with a crude reflector to conceal them from the audience. Some overhead light source would seem necessary, so we may presume at least one large chandelier above the forestage. Behind the proscenium arch there were side-lights, oil lamps on sconces behind the wings, and perhaps another chandelier above the stage area to light the scenery. Although it would strike the modern viewer as odd to have a multi-branched chandelier hanging in the Forest of Arden, or in Brutus's garden as he weighed the fate of Caesar, theatergoers of the time were so accustomed to them that they probably did not even notice.

In sum, the Southwark Theater, while "an ugly, ill-contrived affair" like its sister playhouse in New York, was capable of providing for its Philadelphia patrons a modicum of comfort and, more importantly, of mounting a production with at least as much panache and expertise as its older prototypes in England. It was no Theatre Royal, no Covent Garden or Drury Lane, but it was at least the equivalent of a number of small, provincial town theaters of its day, and probably the superior of many. One has only to look at W. H. Pyne's bitter, accurate drawing "The Country Theatre" to realize that the Southwark was an architectural and artistic asset to eighteenth-century Philadelphia.[27]

Editorial Notes

The Disappointment, as previously noted, was published twice. The first edition, printed in 1767, is used for this volume. The second, extensively revised and expanded by the author, was printed in Philadelphia in 1796, and represents, to my way of thinking, a dilution of the original. Individual speeches are expanded in some cases to the point of tedium, songs are added with even less justification than in the earlier edition, and new and totally extraneous characters are added, to the detriment of the work as a piece of stagecraft. Furthermore, as *The Disappointment* is of primary interest as an historically significant part of the American theater, not as a representative example of the colonial literature of this country, I consider the edition that most closely reproduces what might have been produced on the stage of the Southwark Theater to be of greater value than the later, more literarily self-conscious version.

The copy of the play held by the Library of Congress is very clear and presents few difficulties in transcription. The spelling, capitalization, and punctuation are surprisingly consistent for the period, and there are only two errata. The type used for the printing was obviously new and well set, with sharp definition and strong visual clarity.

I have not tried to reproduce the text of the play precisely; some spellings and punctuation have been modernized. Forrest was rather profligate with commas and extended dashes, and I have tried to systematize his sometimes fanciful punctuation according to modern usage. Overall, my criterion has been readability; where necessary, I have reconstructed the grammar and syntax for the sake of greater understanding by the present-day reader. At no time do I feel I have changed the sense of the lines, nor have I substituted a word to eliminate an archaism. There are no interpretive emendations; the original is too clear to require any. The American spelling of certain words ("show" for "shew," "humor" for "humour," for example) seemed appropriate and has been used throughout. In general I have tried to follow the principle of *res ipse loquitur*.

The ethnic dialogue did present some problems for the editor. Very often Forrest would spell phonetically and occasionally the orthographic variations were useless, e.g., Trushoop's "bote" for "boat," or "cote" for "coat." It served no purpose to retain this peculiarity, so the proper spelling was used in those and a few other instances.

Otherwise I copied the dialect exactly as it was written, in order to give some of the original flavor of the work. Forrest's ear was not very accurate at times—or he may have had difficulty in finding the proper spellings to suggest the accents of his ethnic characters on the printed page. Trushoop's pronunciation of "thief" is written "tief," for example. An Irishman, even on the stage, does not pronounce the "th" sound in this manner; if the pronunciation can be written without recourse to phonetic symbols, the rough aspirate of the initial might be indicated as "t'h-," and the entire word transcribed as "t'hay'f." Nonetheless, I have retained the original spelling of the dialect pronunciations, with the addition of an apostrophe to indicate either an aspirate or a dropped sound.

It is only fair to point out that where Forrest is good, he is very good. The abruptness of the Scotch backclipping is skillfully indicated, and the repetitive Irish rhythms are excellent in the main. Elsewhere I have discussed the particular case of Raccoon; I leave the reader to decide what Forrest's ethnic intent was in this case. For my part I have left the dialogue of Raccoon entirely alone, with the exception of adding apostrophes to indicate dropped sounds or syllables.

I have offered annotations where they would clarify the technical theatrical terms used in the script, or where they would enable the reader to understand the reference in its historical or dramatic contexts. I have presumed no special knowledge of the theater on the part of the reader, nor anything more than a general interest in the history of colonial Philadelphia. Much of the humor of the play lies in its local references, all of which would be recognizable to Philadelphians: where possible I have explained these references in order to indicate a little of the play's particular charm for its time and place.

Notes to the Introduction

1. Most of the information concerning the withdrawal of *The Disappointment* is taken from three sources: George O. Seilhamer, *History of the American Theatre* . . . (Philadelphia, 1888), 1:176–84; John F. Watson, *Annals of Philadelphia and Pennsylvania in the Olden Time* (Philadelphia, 1823), 1:73–74; and John MacPherson, "Letter to William Patterson, May 30, 1767," *Pennsylvania Magazine of History and Biography* 23 (1899):52–53.

2. The production history of the play is drawn in large measure from Hugh S. Rankin, *The Theatre in Colonial America* (Chapel Hill, N.C., 1965), pp. 117–18, as is the majority of the information regarding the career of David Douglass and the American Company of Comedians (chaps. 6–8 passim). Opposition to the theater in general in Philadelphia is well described by Carl and Jessica Bridenbaugh in *Rebels and Gentlemen: Philadelphia in the Age of Franklin* (Oxford, 1942), pp. 135–46.

3. G. B. D. Odell, *Annals of the New York Stage* (New York, 1927), 1:93–95.

4. On the Philadelphia mob, see John C. Miller, *Origins of the American Revolution* (Stanford, 1943), pp. 135–36.

5. Pp. 143–44.

6. The MacPherson letter is referred to in note 1, as is Watson's *Annals*. Forrest's friends are described in Bridenbaugh, p. 127, and in Joseph J. Kelley, Jr., *Life and Times in Colonial Philadelphia* (Harrisburg, 1973), pp. 106–8. For the membership of the Tun Tavern Lodge of Free and Accepted Masons, see PMHB 20 (1896):116–21. Several of the people mentioned in the MacPherson letter as characterized in *The Disappointment* were members of the Lodge: Richard Swan; John Reily; "Yeates a Tavern Keeper," the model for Hum; and Cappock, an instrument-maker, supposedly the model for Quadrant.

7. Rankin is the major source for Douglass's interest in and dependence upon the Masons. See Rankin, p. 28; also pp. 84, 97, 106, 119, 125.

8. For Armbruster, see "C. R. H.," *Notes and Queries*, PMHB 6 (1882):51. See also Abraham H. Cassel, "The German Almanac of Christopher Sauer," PMHB 6 (1882):65, and Townsend Ward, "Second Street and the Second Street Road and Their Associations," PMHB 4 (1880):417. For Armbruster's part in the original hoax, see Watson, p. 73, and Seilhamer, pp. 176–77.

9. The reference to *Douglas* is from Rankin (p. 82), who quotes from an advertisement of the American Company that amply illustrates the lengths to which Douglass was willing to go to gain public approval: "In the announcement [for the production of *Douglas*, Friday, July 13, 1759] he [Douglass] inserted four lines from the original London prologue as a suggestion of the moral virtues of the play:

35

This Night a Douglass [sic], your protection claims:
A Wife! a Mother! Pity's sofest Names:
The Story of her Woes indulgent bear,
And grant your Suppliant all she begs, A TEAR."

For the performance of *Othello* in Rhode Island, see Rankin, p. 94.

10. The production history of *The Prince of Parthia* is told in detail in Seilhamer, 1:185–95. There was an amateur performance of the tragedy at the University of Pennsylvania in 1915. See Arthur Hobson Quinn, *A History of the American Drama from the Beginning to the Civil War* (New York, 1923), pp. 16–17.

11. Concerning the nomination of Leacock, see Dunlap, *History of the American Theatre* . . . (New York, 1832), p. 385. For the Barton reference, see Dunlap, p. 382. Also, see Norman Philbrick, *Trumpets Sounding* (New York, 1972), p. 41, for an intriguing reference to Leacock as the author of *The Disappointment*. Philbrick gives Seilhamer as his source in stating that Leacock wrote *The Disappointment*, whereas Seilhamer states an opinion exactly opposite to the one attributed to him by Philbrick (Seilhamer, 1:184). Regarding John Leacock in general, see Francis James Dallett, Jr., "John Leacock and the Fall of British Tyranny," PMHB 78 (1954):456–75. A seemingly conclusive reference to Forrest as the author of *The Disappointment* is made by Dallett, pp. 470–71*n*. O. G. T. Sonneck's conclusions concerning the authorship of *The Disappointment* come from Dallett, p. 471*n*, and Sonneck, *A Bibliography of Early Secular American Music (18th Century)*, rev. ed., ed. William Treat Upton (New York, 1964), p. 109. See also Sonneck, "Early American Operas," *Sammelbande d. Int. Mus. Ges.* (1904–1905):109.

12. For discussion of Forrest's right to be called the author, see Watson, 1:73–74; Seilhamer, 1:176–84; Bridenbaugh, pp. 127–28; Rankin, pp. 117–18; and Moses Coit Tyler, *Literary History of the American Revolution* (New York, 1897), 2:192*n*. See also Kelley, *Life and Times in Colonial Philadelphia*, pp. 106–8. Kelley is a delightful popular historian, but often inaccurate. He declares, for example, that *The Disappointment* was republished in 1796 as a novel. The major source of information concerning Forrest's life and career is W. A. Newman Dorland, "The Second Troop Philadelphia City Cavalry," PMHB 47 (1923): 371. Forrest's court-martial is recorded for October 3, 1777, in the *Orderly Book of General John Peter Gabriel Muhlenburg, March 26–December 20, 1777*, reprinted in PMHB 35 (1911):75. For details of his postwar career, see Dorland, p. 371, and Thomas H. Shoemaker, "A List of the Inhabitants of Germantown and Chestnut Hill in 1809," PMHB 15 (1891):471. Forrest's participation in the Battle of Trenton and the admonishment by General Washington are described breathlessly by Howard Fast, *The Crossing* (New York, 1971), pp. 146–47. His involvement in the "Great Philadelphia Balloon Hoax" is suggested unconvincingly by Joseph Jackson, "The First Balloon Hoax," PMHB 35 (1911):51–58. The Lafayette anecdote may be found in Samuel Breck, "A Collection of Puns and Witticisms of Judge Richard Peters," PMHB 25 (1901):369. See also Jacob Mordecai, "Addenda to Watson's Annals," ed. Whitfield J. Bell, PMHB 98 (1974):138; Townsend Ward, "The Germantown Road and its Associations," PMHB 9 (1882):6; *Notes and Queries*, PMHB 4 (1880):121; W. W. H. Davis,

"Washington on the West Bank of the Delaware, 1776," PMHB 4 (1880):154; Benjamin M. Nead, "A Sketch of General Thomas Proctor," PMHB 4 (1880): 457; Benjamin Marshall, "Letter to His Wife, September 12, 1777," PMHB 17 (1893):341; *Norristown Herald*, March 23, 1825; "The Orderly Book of the Second Pennsylvania Continental Line," PMHB 35 (1911):465–85; and *Weekly Magazine* (Philadelphia), March 31, 1798, p. 285, and April 7, 1798, p. 316.

13. *The Beggar's Opera* went through thirteen editions (four of them pirated) by 1750. For this, see George H. Nettleton and Arthur E. Case, eds., *British Dramatists from Dryden to Sheridan* (Boston, 1939), p. 937.

14. Seilhamer, 1:179.

15. Rankin, p. 117.

16. "Raccoon: 2. (*fig.*) A member of the New Jersey militia in the American Revolution. 1779 N. J. Archives 2 Ser. III. 703: 'Each *devoted raccoon* (is) to receive down forty *soft* or *paper* dollars.'" In *A Dictionary of American English*, ed. Sir William A. Craigie and James R. Hulbert (Chicago, 1942), vol. 3. On Raccoon Point, New Jersey, see PMHB 74 (1950):502.

17. Seilhamer, 1:178–79.

18. This point is developed extensively in Allardyce Nicoll, *A History of Early Eighteenth Century Drama, 1700–1750* (Cambridge, 1929); see esp. chap. 4. See also Edmond M. Gagey, *Ballad Opera* (New York, 1937).

19. Seilhamer, 1:184. Seilhamer gives no reasons or justification for his choices, although they seem to be logical, in view of the information we have about the acting abilities of the members of the American Company. Further speculative research in the area of tentative casting needs to be done, particularly for this period.

20. Rankin is my main source for this summary of the theatrical activities of the Hallam and Douglass troupes. See his *Theatre in Colonial America*, chaps. 5, 6, and 8. See also Kelley, p. 113.

21. The unimpressed visitor to the Southwark signed himself "Lang Syne" and is quoted in Watson, *Annals of Philadelphia . . .*, 1:473. The outside dimensions of the Southwark are taken from Brooks MacNamara, *The American Playhouse in the Eighteenth Century* (Cambridge, Mass., 1969), p. 52. Most of the information we have about the theaters in colonial America has been collected by MacNamara in this remarkable work. The cost of the Southwark is from Mac-Namara, p. 52. For Douglass's new scenery see *South Carolina Gazette* (Charleton), October 30, 1766.

22. For this speculative reconstruction of the auditorium of the Southwark I depended upon MacNamara, pp. 47–49, 54. See also Mordecai, "Addenda to Watson's Annals," PMHB 98 (1974):157.

23. Again, MacNamara (pp. 56–58) provides much of the data on lighting in the Southwark.

24. This description of the stage and proscenium is from MacNamara, p. 43 et seq.; Richard Southern, *The Georgian Playhouse* (London, 1948); Garff B. Wilson, *Three Hundred Years of American Drama and Theatre* (Englewood Cliffs, N.J., 1973), pp. 19–27; and Oscar G. Brockett, *History of the Theatre* (Boston, 1968), pp. 272–73. The inscription on the proscenium at Plumsted's warehouse translates: "All the World plays the Actor."

25. Scenic practices in the eighteenth-century English playhouse are best described by Richard Southern, *Changeable Scenery: Its Origin and Development in the British Theatre* (London, 1962), to which this description is heavily indebted. The cost of the scenery for the Society Hill theater is from MacNamara, p. 47.

26. The special effects at the Southwark are from MacNamara, p. 67. The split-stage method of staging is described by MacNamara, p. 66.

27. See MacNamara, p. 19.

THE
DISAPPOINTMENT,

OR, THE
FORCE OF CREDULITY

A NEW

AMERICAN COMIC-OPERA

Of Two ACTS

by ANDREW BARTON, Esq;

Enchanting gold! that doth conspire to blind
Man's erring judgment, and misguide the mind;
In search of thee, the wretched worldling goes;
Nor danger fears, tho' FIENDS of night oppose.[1]

NEW YORK

Printed in the Year, M,DCC,LXVII

The Author's

PREFACE TO THE PUBLIC[2]

The following local piece, entitled *The Disappointment, or the Force of Credulity* was originally written for my own and the amusement of a few particular friends who, unknown to me, were pleased to signify their approbation of it in such a manner that it soon engrossed the chief part of the conversation of all ranks of people, who expressed their desire to hear it and have it published. Under these circumstances, I was greatly at a loss how to proceed: I did not choose (as I saw no merit in it) to expose it to the criticism of critics, to put it in the power of gentlemen skilled in scholastic knowledge, to ridicule my ignorance or condescend to the intreaties of those who I thought had no more sense than myself and who might, perhaps, have made it better than it really is. Conscious therefore of my own inability, I determined to excuse myself to all, and in this determination I persisted for some time, but at last, for my own safety was obliged to capitulate and surrender on the following stipulations: first, the infrequency of dramatic compositions in America, secondly, the torrent of solicitations from all quarters, thirdly, the necessity of contributing to the entertainment of the city, fourthly and lastly, to put a stop (if possible) to the foolish and pernicious practice of searching after supposed hidden treasure.* These terms, hard as they are, I have with reluctance been forced to submit to. I am therefore obliged in vindication of my conduct to assure the

---

*Many people to this day are possessed with an idle notion of the pirates burying money up or down the riverside, and are so infatuated with the hopes of obtaining it that they neglect their business by day with the thoughts of it, by which their families suffer, and at night, like so many mischievous muskrats spoil the pastures and bank along shore to the very great annoyance of their industrious neighbors. *Quere*, is this not insufferable? And ought not these injured people to petition for an act entitled, An act to prevent this unconstitutional digging act from being any longer in force as an act, with a heavy fine on those two-legged muskrats. And should they refuse or be incapable of paying it, that they should be deprived of what is most valuable in a muskrat, to be sold for the benefit of the sufferers.[3]

41

public that the story is founded on matter of fact, transacted near the city not long since, and recent in the memory of thousands; for the truth of which assertion I appeal to numbers of my fellow citizens. But in order to give strangers and those unacquainted with the story some idea of it the following short history is thought necessary: the scheme was planned by four humorous gentlemen, Hum, Parchment, Quadrant, and Rattletrap, to divert themselves and friends and try what lengths credulity and the love of money would carry men. In order to put their scheme into execution they framed a plausible, well-connected story of hidden treasure and to gloss the matter, adapted sundry papers to their purpose and pitched upon two suitable old fellows, Washball and Raccoon, as principal dupes with others, to try the success of their scheme, which had the desired effect.

The moral shows the folly of an over-credulity and desire of money and how apt men are—especially old men—to be unwarily drawn into schemes where there is but the least shadow of gain and concludes with these observations; that mankind ought to be contented with their respective stations, to follow their vocations with honesty and industry—the only sure way to gain riches.

I do not figure to myself the least advantage accruing from it but the inward satisfaction of contributing my mite to stop the current of such folly. Such as it is I submit to the public for their sanction or condemnation, and if any merit should appear in the performance I shall not vainly attribute it to myself, but give the credit of it to mere chance.

> I am the public's
> most obedient,
> most devoted and
> most faithful humble
> servant,
> Andrew Barton

PROLOGUE[4]

Though distant far from famed Britannia's isle,
Where comic scenes call cynics forth to smile;
Our artless muse hath made her first essay
T'intrust and please you with a modern play.
Theatric business was, and still should be,
To point out vice in its deformity;
Make virtue fair shine eminently bright,
Rapture the breast and captivate the sight.
No matter which, the pulpit or the stage,
Condemn the vice and folly of the age;
These are our boasts, and on sure ground we stand,
Plead virtue's cause throughout this infant land;
We mount the stage and lend a helping hand.
Wit, fools, a knave and conjurer tonight,
The objects make both of your ears and sight.
A band of dupes are humm'd with idle schemes,
Quit solid sense for airy golden dreams.
Our flattering muse thinks she's some merit gained,
Pursuing truth, and things (like truth) well feigned.
The subject's suited to our present times,
No person's touched, although he lash their crimes;
Nor gall or copp'ras tincture her design,[5]
But gay good humor breathe in every line.
If you condemn her—she for censure stands;
But if applaud—then thundering clap your hands.

DRAMATIS PERSONAE[6]

Men

Hum
Parchment
Quadrant
Rattletrap, a supposed conjurer.
Raccoon, an old debauchee.
Washball, an avaricious old barber.
Trushoop, a cooper.
McSnip, a tailor.
Meanwell, a gentleman, in love with *Washball's* niece.
Topinlift, a sailor.
Spitfire, an assistant to *Rattletrap*.

Women

Moll Placket, a woman of the town, in keeping by *Raccoon*.
Mrs. Trushoop, wife to *Trushoop*.
Miss Lucy, Washball's niece, in love with *Meanwell*.

Collector, Blackbeard's Ghost, Tailors, Servants, *etc.*

THE DISAPPOINTMENT,

OR, THE FORCE OF CREDULITY

ACT ONE.

SCENE ONE: A Tavern.

(*Scene opens and discovers Hum, Parchment and Quadrant seated around a table with wine, etc.*)[7]
(*Parchment, pouring out a glass of wine, sings,* "Sing tantara, rara, rogues all, rogues all, sing tantara, rara, rogues all.")

Parchment

Come, success to us.
(*Drinks. All drink.*)
Well, gentlemen! How goes our scheme? Have you made any new proselytes since our last meeting?

Hum

Why, really, while credulity and the love of money prevail, I think it no merit to make proselytes of one-half the town. But that you know is not our purpose. We only want to draw in four or five. I baited the hook for the old shaver; he gaped, snapped and swallowed it as voraciously as a cringing courtier would a pension. As for Raccoon, I just threw out a few hints. He soon discovered the foundation, and raised the fabric himself.

Quadrant

Oh, if he smells money, as great a coward as they say he is, he'll venture to the gates of hell for it. Ha, ha, ha.

Hum

I've hitherto kept him in suspense. He haunts me like a ghost. He thinks something, but knows nothing. He'll be here presently, and I have contrived matters so that he shall make the discovery himself.

47

Quadrant

So far we have sailed before the wind, and I've not been idle, for I've drawn in Trushoop and McSnip.[8] They've been with me these three nights consulting proper measures for obtaining the treasure, and are so elevated that I'm afraid they'll run crazy. Ha, ha, ha! Trushoop speaks of building a chapel at his own expense and employing a score of priests to keep up a continual rotation of prayers for the repose of the souls of those poor fellows who buried it.[9] As for McSnip, he intends to knock off business, home to England and purchase a title. Ha, ha, ha! They'll both be here in half an hour.

Parchment

The devil they do! Then I suppose they'll not be in a humor for work 'till this affair is over. I'd some thoughts for a new suit of clothes, but I must drop them 'till these chimeras are out of McSnip's brain.

Hum

That's one reason why I want the business dispatched. For, though I like the diversion, I wouldn't hurt their families. Mr. Parchment, have you prepared the papers?

Parchment

Yes, yes, I have 'em here in my pocket.

Quadrant

Do let's see 'em. Ha, ha, ha! For they are the foundation of all our undertaking.

Parchment

(*Pulling out the papers.*)
Here they are, all placed in regular order, and enclosed in a letter to Mr. Hum.

Hum

Aye, aye. Let's see.
(*Reads.*)
The letter will do to a tittle—but what the devil's this?
(*Taking hold of the parchment.*)

Parchment

That's the will.

Hum

Why, it looks as if it had been preserved in the Temple of Apollo, or the Tower of Babel.

Quadrant

Egad, you might have said Noah's ark—ha,ha,ha!—for it looks old enough. And pray, what's this old weather-beaten piece?

Parchment

Why, that's the draught of the place where the treasure lies, together with the memorandum signed by all present at the time it was deposited.

Quadrant

Ha, ha, ha! Droll enough.

(*Sings.*)

Air I. "I am a brisk young lively lass."

In all the town there's none like you,
When you're on mischief bent, sirs:
With pen and ink one well can write,
What you do both invent, sirs.
It's you, my boys, it's you can do it,
Parchment, you are my darling.
Raccoon may curse, and Washball burst,
We value not their snarling. Tol, lol, etc.

Hum

Well, I must take these into my care, as they are directed to me.

(*Gathers up the papers.*)

But I wonder what detains Jack Rattletrap?

Quadrant

Oh, I'll be bound for his appearance. I was at his house just now, and found him pouring over the canto of Hudibras and Sydrophel in order to furnish himself with a set of hard words which, added to his knowledge in the mathematics, will sufficiently qualify him for a modern conjurer.[10] But here he comes! Ha, ha, ha!—talk of the devil and his imps appear.

(*Enter Rattletrap, singing.*)

Air II. "The Bloom of May."

Behold you my magic phiz,
How solemn and grave I look;

> Here, here, my good friends, here is
>   My brassbound magical book.
> This book wonders contain,
>   'Twould deceive the devil himself,
> And puzzle a conjurer's brain,
>   That knows no more than myself. That knows, *etc.*
> Your servant, gentlemen.
> (*All say*, "Your servant, Mr. Rattletrap.")

Quadrant

Take your chair. Come, sir, my service to you.
(*All drink.*)

Parchment

We began to look for you with impatience. Well, are you almost prepared for your office?

Rattletrap

Yes, dress and books are already provided, but for tools I must apply to Mr. Quadrant.

Quadrant

Yes, yes. I'll cut you a hazel-rod off our cherry tree, a magnet, nocturnal and forestaff shall all be ready.[11] And I can furnish you, as Hudibras says, with a
> "Moon dial, and Napier's bones,
> With store of constellation stone."[12]
Ha, ha, ha! But say, have you seen the papers?

Rattletrap

Yes, I saw them this morning at Mr. Parchment's office. But, hark'ee, we want a fifth person to act as demi-devil, or familiar spirit.

Hum

Leave that to me. I am acquainted with an old artilleryman—he's a snug, dry dog—I'll introduce him to you. With his assistance and a proper habit, you'll cut as droll a figure as old Merlin.

Rattletrap

Well, well, but we must have a place provided for his reception, underground. Mr. Quadrant and I will see that done—drop the conversation, here comes old Raccoon.
(*Enter Raccoon.*)

Raccoon
> Your servant, gentlemen. Broder Hum, I'm bery glad to see you.[13]
> Mr. Quadrant, Mr. Parchment, Mr. Rattletrap.
> (*He salutes them all.*)

Parchment
> Leave ceremonies, and take hold of the bottle.
> (*All drink.*)

Hum
> Brother Raccoon, and gentlemen all, I must beg your patience for
> a few minutes. I'll be with you instantly.
> (*Exit.*)
> (*As he goes out, he drops the papers; Raccoon picks them up, steps
> aside and looks them over.*)

Raccoon
> (*Aside.*)[14]
> Ah, broder Hum, have I found your secret? I t'ought dere was
> something in de wind—dis is a lucky bout—now, my dream's out.
> Dad, I'll keep dese papers—dey shan't hab dem, unless I gets de
> share.
> (*He crams them into his bosom.*)

Parchment
> Come, Mr. Raccoon, sit down.
> (*Raccoon sits down.*)
> (*Re-enter Hum.*)

Hum
> Did you see anything of a bundle of papers, gentlemen?

Parchment
> No, I saw none.

Quadrant
> Nor I. You didn't leave them here.

Hum
> Speak, gentlemen—if you've got them, pray don't keep me in sus-
> pense.

Rattletrap
> Upon my honor, I saw nothing of 'em.

Hum

Pray put me out of my pain, gentlemen.
(*They all rise, shake their clothes and look about for them.*)
If they are not here, the damned drawer must have picked my
pocket when he brought up the wine. Damn the villain!
(*He knocks.*)[15]

Drawer

(*Below.*)
Coming, sir!
(*Enter Drawer.*)

Drawer

Sir, here's some gentlemen.
(*Enter Washball, Trushoop and McSnip.*)

Hum

(*Locks the door and speaks to the drawer.*)
You scoundrel, where's the papers you took?

Drawer

Sir, I didn't take any.

Hum

You lie, you rascal!

Washball

What's the matter? What's the matter, neighbor Hum?

Hum

We're ruined, Mr. Washball—the villain has stolen the papers!

Washball

Deliver the papers! Deliver the papers, you dog!

Drawer

Upon my honor, gentlemen! I didn't see any.

Trushoop

Damn your honor, you t'ief! I hope it's no defence, gentlemen.

McSnip

'Onor! What, a drawer in a tayvirn have 'onor?

Washball

You lie, you lie, you dog!
(*He lifts up his cane to strike him.*)

Quadrant

His countenance condemns him.

Drawer

Indeed, indeed, gentlemen, I saw no papers at all!

Hum

You rascal! You've got 'em! I'll send for a constable immediately.

Drawer

For God's sake, gentlemen!

Trushoop

Oh, you t'ief of the world! When I fish for the devil I'll bait my hook wid you.

McSnip

'Gin I come to him, I'll cut his thro't.

Drawer

Oh, Lord! Oh, Lord!

McSnip

Produce the pappers this enstant, or by St. Andra' I'll sacrefeese ye![16]
(*He seizes and shakes him.*)

Drawer

Oh, Lord! Gentlemen, have mercy! Don't kill me!

Washball

Kill the dog, kill him.
(*He strikes at him with his cane.*)

Drawer

(*On his knees.*)
As I hope for mercy, I'm innocent, gentlemen!

McSnip

You've but one moment to live. Deliver, or I'll—

Raccoon

Come, gentlemen! Be merciful. Don't kill de poor fellow—search him.
(*They search him and find none.*)

Hum

They're not about him. What shall we do? Come, come, my lad. Look'ee—be ingenuous with us—they're of no service to you, and if you'll produce 'em in half an hour we'll give you something handsome. Perhaps I've dropped them. Do, my lad, step down and look about.

Drawer

I will, sir, and make what search I can.
(*Exit Drawer.*)

Raccoon

Come, come, make yourselves easy, gentlemen. I did pick up de papers at de door. Broder Hum dropped dem as he went out. I see de contents of dem—here dey are. And I hope, gentlemen, dat you will let me come in for the share.
(*He gives the papers.*)
(*All say,* "Agreed, agreed, agreed.")

Hum

We always intended you should have a share, brother Raccoon. Well, now the papers are safe we're all right again. Come, sit down, gentlemen. Very lucky! Very lucky, indeed!
(*All sit down.*)

Parchment

(*To Washball.*)
What can these papers mean?

Washball

Oh, dear! Oh dear, how my heart beats for joy!

Trushoop

So do mine. I t'ought it would t'ump my liver out.

McSnip

An' I had no' been stopped, I should 'a' cut his thro't—I'm glad you prevented me. Let's call him up and ge' him samthing.

Hum

Aye, aye, by all means.
(*He knocks.*)
(*Re-enter Drawer.*)

Drawer

Did you call, gentlemen?

McSnip

Weel, lad, we've foond the pappers, and here's samthing to mak'
ye ameends for the freeght ye got.
(*He gives him money.*)
And meend ye tall na' ane, but keep it to yoursel'.

Drawer

Thank'ee kindly, sir! God bless you, sir. Thank you, kind sir.
(*Bowing.*)

Washball

Aye, aye, a close tongue makes a wise head. Remember that, young
man.
(*Exit Drawer.*)

Parchment

(*To Trushoop.*)
I say, Mr. Trushoop, what are the contents of these papers?

Trushoop

The devil a hair I know about it at all, at all.

Hum

Well, gentlemen, I look upon you all to be men of honor—I suppose you're not strangers to the business at hand. You've all been
informed of it, except brother Raccoon and Mr. Parchment, who
are both present and shall soon be informed.

Parchment

(*Starting up suddenly.*)
Gentlemen! I expected when I was sent for here that I was to
meet, as usual, to take a cheerful glass with my old friends.[17] I
knew of no secret to be divulged—not I—and I earnestly request,
that if it is any scheme, plot, combination, rout, riot, or unlawful
assembly—in fine, if it is anything against his most sacred majesty,
George the Second, of Great Britain, France and Ireland King, De-
fender of the Faith, *etc.*, whom God preserve![18] Or the lords of his
majesty's most honorable privy council, or any one of them, or the
lords spiritual or temporal, or either of them, or the honorable the

House of Commons of Great Britain—that standing bulwark of
British freedom—or either of them. The Lord-Lieutenant or Parliament of Ireland, or either of them. The Church of England as
by law established, or the government under which we live—I say,
gentlemen, if it is any scheme, plot, combination, rout, riot or unlawful assembly as aforesaid, keep it to yourself—don't let me
know a tittle of it. I wash my hands of it for, if I know it I'll be a
swift witness against you! For as I hope to be saved I'll immediately
to the attorney-general, lodge an information against you and hang
you every mother's son!

Washball

Dear, dear sir! Mr. Parchment, don't think of such a thing.

Parchment

Don't tell me, sir!

Washball

Sir, you've known me these many, many years—I've lived peace-
ably and never was concerned in any of these disturbances you
mentioned.

Parchment

Mr. Washball, I've nothing to charge you with, but sir, my sus-
picions are—

Washball

Lord! Lord! Sir, sir!

Rattletrap

Sir, I believe there's no one in this company but has as much
loyalty as yourself.

McSnip

By my saul, mon! I ha' as great a regord to the illustreus hoose of
Hanover as ye ha'.[19]

Parchment

It may be so, sir.

Quadrant

I'm surprised at you, Mr. Parchment.

Trushoop

The devil burn me but so am I, too.

Raccoon

Come, come, Mr. Parchment—consider—

Hum

I hope, Mr. Parchment, you don't suppose any of us capable of conspiring against his majesty or his government—No sir, I answer for myself: his majesty hath not a more loyal subject. The whole business that you were desired to attend upon here I'll instantly communicate, if you'll hear. But if not, sir—

Washball

Aye, do hear, do hear, Mr. Parchment.

Trushoop

Arra, my dear, and have a little patience, and we'll tell you all, and more, too.[20]

Parchment

If it is none of these things, gentlemen, I have mentioned, I am ready to hear.

Hum

Well, then, you must know that I have very unexpectedly, and to my very great joy, received a letter from my loving sister-in-law—who is heir to the famous Captain Blackbeard—enclosing sundry papers such as plans, drafts, and memorandums of a great quantity of treasure that was buried by the pirates. Here are the papers, gentlemen, please to look them over.[21]

(*Pulling them out of his pocket: they look over them.*)

Parchment

I beg your pardon, gentlemen. Since it's an affair of this nature, I join you with all my heart.

Trushoop

The devil doubt you, my dear honey.

Raccoon

(*Pointing to one of the papers in Parchment's hand.*)
What's dat? Do, Mr. Parchment, read it. I can't see widout my spectacles.

Parchment

Why, I find—but I'll omit the preamble—it's a particular account of the treasure, which I'll read. Imprimis, seventeen golden candlesticks, chalices and crucifixes; thirty thousand Portugal pieces, twenty thousand Spanish pistoles, four hundred and seventy thousand pistereens, seventy-three bars of gold, a small box of diamonds, sixty thousand pieces-of-eight and one hundred and fifty pounds weight of gold-dust.[22] This instrument was signed by Edward Teach, alias Blackbeard, captain, Moses Brimstone, first lieutenant, Bryan Fireball, second lieutenant, Judas Guzzlefire, gunner, and Jeffery Eatdevil, cook.[23]

Washball

Oh, what a treasure! What do you think of our plot now, Mr. Parchment? Ha, ha, ha!

Parchment

I like it extremely well, sir. I wish I had been concerned in such a plot twenty years ago.

Trushoop

The devil a word a lie in all that again, oh hon'acree.[24]

Hum

Aye! Well, here's enough for us all.

Trushoop

By my shoul! It's a very fine sight if a body could but feel it.

McSnip

By my saul, I'll awa' wi' all me dranken joorneymen, and keck the shap-boord oot 'a' the wandow.[25]

Washball

I'll shave no more—no, not I—I'll keep my hands out of the suds.

Raccoon

Dis will make me cut de proper figure in life, and appear in the world wid the proper impo'tance. And den I'll do somet'ing for my poor friend.

Rattletrap

Our business must be carried on with secrecy and dispatch. Besides, it will be attended with some expense. I believe, gentlemen, it will be necessary to appoint Mr. Parchment our secretary and treasurer, if it is agreeable to him.
(*All say*, "With all our hearts.")

Parchment

Gentlemen, you have already laid me under many obligations, and this appointment I look upon as a further proof of your esteem. I accept it with gratitude, and heartily thank you for your kind information and the great confidence you have reposed in me. And you may depend upon the utmost secrecy, faithfulness, accuracy, dispatch and punctuality.

Trushoop

Fait', my dear, that's a very fine spache, by me showl! Father Duffy never made a better.[26]

Quadrant

Mr. Rattletrap, what do you imagine will be the expense to each individual?

Rattletrap

Oh, trifling, trifling. I suppose about two pistoles a man.[27]

Washball

Well, I've money about me—I may as well pay it now. Here, Mr. Parchment, is a doubloon for my neighbor Trushoop and myself.

Trushoop

Mashah, my dear! And I'm very much obliged to you.[28]

Rattletrap

Before I make use of my art to discover this treasure, I must insist that each individual of you go to Mr. Parchment's office and be sworn to secrecy and honesty to each other, and you who have not paid, leave your respective quotas.
(*All say,* "Agreed, agreed.")

Hum

Well, gentlemen, it grows late, we'll break up. I expect to see you all tomorrow at six. Meanwhile, let it remain a profound secret. Remember, we're now going to be sworn, so don't let your wives or nearest friends know it.
(*They all rise.*)

Parchment

(*Sings.*)
Air III. "How Blessed Has my Time Been."
    Now let us join hands and unite in this cause;

'Tis glorious gold that will gain us applause.
How blessed now are we, with such treasure in store,
We'll clothe all the naked and feed all the poor.
    We'll clothe all, *etc.*
                            II
How happy for me to this country I came,
You all, my dear friends, now can witness the same.
In wealth to abound—oh! the thought is most sweet,
No more will I write for one farthing a sheet.
    No more, *etc.*

McSnip

Now, my bra'e lad, let's aw stand true.

Trushoop

Arra, fait'! We will, that's true for you.
(*Exeunt.*)

                SCENE TWO: A Street.

(*Enter Trushoop.*)

Trushoop

Now and what the devil will I say to my wife? Or what excuse
will I make. By my showl, she looked wery black at me t'oder
night, when I came home in the morning. By the Holy Stone, I'm
very 'fraid to knock at the dure[29]—But I can't stand this way, lying
out in the cowld all night. By my showl, this s'hitting up all night
will be the de't' of me. Fait', I'll tell her all the sacret—but that
won't do nather, for I'm booksworn. I'll not sell my showl to the
devil for a few scowldings. Well, if I had the wasdom of the holy
Saint Dominick, Saint Patrick, Saint Kullumkill and all the pious
saints of Ireland, I wouldn't be able to tell f'at to do—But, fait',
I must come in somehow or t'oder.[30]
(*Knocks at the door.*)

Mrs. Trushoop

(*At the window.*)
Who's there?

Trushoop

Who else, my dare, but your own Trushoop? Open the dure, if
you please, my dare.

Mrs. Trushoop

Not I, by my conscience! Go to the hoores where you came from! I'll not be disturbed this way by you every night.

Trushoop

Open the dure, my dare, if you plaze. The nabours will make a great talk, my dare, if you don't, for nabour Glibtongue's paple are all up.

Mrs. Trushoop

F'at do I care for the nabours? They know I'm an honest, vartuous woman—and that's all they can say of me. It's no matters how soon they know of your goings-on—if you stay out every night 'till day.

Trushoop

Well, if you won't open it, my dear, yourself, why then call Tarance, if you please.

Mrs. Trushoop

Indeed, and I call no Tarance! If you want Tarance, why, call him yourself. I'll not be staying up in the cowld, killing my life this way, so I won't.
(*She retires from the window.*)

Trushoop

(*Knocks at the door.*)
Tarance! Tarance, Tarance!

Terence

(*Within, answers.*)
coming, sir!

Trushoop

Well, then, come away, and—fait'!—you and I will go to work togeder, so we will—For by my showl! the shap will be the stillesht plaashe in the howshe for me, for I'd rader hare the cooper's march than the sound of my wife's tongue the day.[31]
(*Knocks again.*)
Tarance!

Terence

(*Within.*)
Coming.

Trushoop

Augh! Dis oat'! Dis day will be a bad night for me. Well, the devil
a hair do I care! F'en I get the money, she'll soon make it up wid
me, for I'll make her as great as the Earl of Portleydown's own
wife. Lady Barrymoore hersalf shan't be finer den she.[32]
(*Knocks again and calls.*)
Tarance! Why, you t'ief of the world, if you don't come down in
a minute, I'll give shelaley! Why, Tarance—

Terence

(*Within the door.*)
I'm just here.

Trushoop

By my showl! This fellow is enough to weary the pashence of Saint
Ignatius or the Holy Pope himself—Tarance![33]

Terence

(*Opens the door and enters the street.*)
Shure, I'm just here.

Trushoop

You t'ief of the world! Why didn't you let me in when I t'umped?

Terence

(*Scratching his head and grumbling.*)
Shure, if you comed home in time we'd not have all this noise, so
we wouldn't.

Trushoop

Give us none of your gum, you spalpeen of perdition! By my
showl, I'll give you shelaley, so I would.
(*He beats him, Terence bawls aloud.*)

Terence

Oh! Murder! Murder! Master dare, don't kill one.

Mrs. Trushoop

(*Returns to the window.*)
Aren't you ashamed to be making a great noise all night in the
strate this morning, and killing the poor boy for nothing?

Terence

Arra, mistress dare, spake to him—Master, dare, laave off, for
shure I was aslape when I heard you call.

Trushoop

(*Pushes Terence from him and says:*)
To the devil I pitch all liars! Go to your work, you t'ief of the
world, and if you don't make me five tight kaggs this day that will
hold no vater I'll bate you so long as I'm able and longer, too.
(*They cross the stage and exeunt.*)

SCENE THREE: A Room
in Moll Placket's House.

(*Enter Raccoon with a spit, pick-axe and spade.*)

Raccoon

What shall I do wid dese things? Dad, I'll put dem under the
bed.[34]
(*He steps into the next room, puts them under the bed and returns.*)
But, where's Mrs. Placket? She'll be oberjoyed when I tell her—
Dad, I'll dress her off as fine as de Queen of Sheba, when she come
to see broder Solomon.[35] She shall go to de play ebery night, a
coach and two footmen to attend her. Do' I'm an old man, dad!
I've streng't in the back and marrow in de bone, and as bigorous
as some young fellows of twenty-five—dat Mrs. Placket can
testify.
(*He calls.*)
Placket? Pet? Pet?

Placket

(*Within.*)[36]
Pet's a'coming, pet's a'coming, dear Coony—
(*Enter Placket.*)
Here's pet.

Raccoon

Buss me, my dear, and I'll tell you somet'ing dat will make you
happy.

Placket

What, is your wife dead? Say—tell me—for I know that will make
us happy.

Raccoon

No, but it's bery near so good—but you'll tell.

Placket

No, indeed, indeed, indeed I won't, my dear Coony.

Raccoon

Well, den, I'll not keep my dear pet in suspense any longer. But you must buss me when I say anyt'ing dat pleases you.

Placket

Well . . . so I will, then.

Raccoon

Well, den—Mr. Hum had receibed a letter from his sister in England wid an account of two or t'ree hundred thousand pound dat was buried by old Blackbeard de pirate, wid the draft where it is hid. And we know de bery spot.
(*She kisses him.*)
And I'll gib you five hundred pound a year for pin-money—
(*She kisses him.*)
and we'll ride in de coach togeder—
(*Kisses.*)
and we'll go to de play togeder—
(*Kisses.*)
and den we'll come home and go to bed togeder—
(*Kisses.*)
and den we'll—ah, you little rogue, you!
(*Kisses again.*)

Placket

And do you really think you'll find it? Why, if you knew where all the treasure in the world was buried, you'd never obtain it without a conjurer.

Raccoon

Yes, my dear, but we hab a conjurer—we'b got Mr. Rattletrap. He understands 'strology and de magic art better den any man in the guberment—and dis night we intend to make de trial—and I must go dis instant and settle de place of meeting.

Placket

Can you leave me so soon, my dear Coony?
(*Raccoon sings.*)

Air IV. "Yankee Doodle."[37]
>Oh, how joyful shall I be,
>>When I get de money,
>I will bring it all to dee;
>>Oh, my diddling honey.

(*Exit, singing the chorus*, "Yankee doodle, *etc.*")

Placket

Bye bye, Coony!—There he goes, and good luck attend him. Poor old fool, he thinks I have a prodigious fondness for him—and so I have for his better part, that's his money. He has been deficient for sometime past, but he thinks he makes that up with soft language, for he calls me his pet, his dove, his "poor t'ing," and a thousand such soft names. And I keep pace with him as well I can, for I call him Coony, cock-a-pigeon, sugar-plum, cock-a-dandy and all the sweet things I can think of. Was anyone to overhear us, they'd think we were two little children playing baby—and we really do but little more—But thank fortune I'm not at a loss for a friend to make up his deficiency, though he thinks me as innocent as a dove. And indeed I'm like a dove in one respect, for when I lose one mate I mourn 'till I get another. But I hope the worst is past.

(*She sings.*)

Air V. "Shambuy."
>Though I hate the old wretch, full as bad as Jack Ketch,
>>My necessities tell me to please him.
>I will ogle and whine 'till I make his gold mine,
>>For that's the best method to ease him.
>I'll simper and leer, and I'll call him my dear,
>>And be loving as ever I can be,
>Then hasten, old Coony, and fetch me the money,
>>For that will exact to my plan be.

(*Exit, singing the chorus*, "laral, *etc.*")

SCENE FOUR: A Street.

(*Enter Rattletrap and Quadrant, meeting Hum.*)

Hum

Hey, Mr. Rattletrap! Which way?

Rattletrap

I'm just returned from the place of action. We go on gloriously! Quadrant and I must set out half an hour before the rest to set all things in readiness. I've left Spitfire there and given him his proper cue.

Hum

What do ye think? Ha, ha—I just now saw brother Raccoon with a long catalogue of his military achievements both in Jamaica and on the continent, together with a treatise he wrote on military discipline last war for the instruction not only of our militia officer, but the regular officers likewise.—The same that he sent to the coffee-house—you remember it? I could scarcely forbear laughing while he was explaining "de hollow square," and "de ebolutions," as he calls it. He's gone in great haste to lay 'em before the governor, to procure his recommendation to the secretary of state for a colonel's commission. I find nothing less than a regiment will satisfy him, which he thinks his merit alone entitles him to. But whether or not, he swears he'll make his gold subservient to his ambitions when he obtains it.

Quadrant

Bravo! Ha, ha, ha!

Hum

I'm at a loss to know how he's to bear up under his disappointment. Sure nothing can equal his folly but his vanity. But, I'm in great hopes this experiment will cure him.

Rattletrap

No matter how much he's disappointed, I'm doubtful fellows of his turn are incapable of proper reflection.

Hum

True. But it's a great pity for all. Well, remember we're all to meet at the Ton precisely at six.[38]
(*Looks at his watch.*)
We've but half an hour to spare. Adieu, adieu.
(*Exeunt.*)

SCENE FIVE: A Tailor's Shop.

(*Tailors at work, some singing and some whistling. Enter McSnip, with his broad-sword.*)

McSnip

Awa', awa' wi' ye aw! Awa'! Begone, ye scoondrels! Oot o' my hoose this minute, or by Saint Andra' I'll chop the heeds off every vullain o' ye. Oot, ye vele scum! No' a word oot o' your heed, or I'se mak' a sacrefeeze o' ye aw'.

(*He makes a cut at the brass knob on the door with his broadsword, and cuts it off. The tailors all run off the shop board in confusion, tumbling over one another, with their stockings about their heels.*)

Nae mair my hoose will be a resaptacle for thieves, ye prackloose sins o' hoores! These thirty years past I'se been a sleeve to ye aw'. Awa', awa' ste'tepe, bookrum, mooneer, guze, shares and aw!³⁹

(*He kicks and throws them about the stage.*)

Na' mair accasion ha' I for ye! Now I'se cleared the shap boord, the naxt thing is to clear all o' its rubbage.

(*Kicks the skirts of cloth and rags about the stage.*)

I'll sot up this rume for the resaption of jontlemen o' the foorst ronk, then gang to Breetain, buy a teetle and occept a pleece at court. It shall be nawthing less than Loord Chaumberlin, or Meester of the Waardrobe—than I'll be a gude freend to America.⁴⁰ And now I've eased my meend o' the parplaxity o' buzness —now for the trazure. I'll gang and mate my company.

(*Sings.*)

Air VI. "The Bonny Broom."

> I'se cut out political cloth,
>   To patch and mend the state;
> My bodkin and my thimble both,
>   Combine to make me great.
> I'se meesured oot a pleece at court,
>   That best with grandeur suits;
> I'se scorn ane of the meaner sort,
>   Like silly paltry brutes.
> Oh, the gold, the bonny, bonny gold!
>   That's buried near the mill;

>Oh, could I get ane grip of thee,
>Then I should ha' my will.

(*Exit.*)

SCENE SIX: A Room in Washball's House.

(*Enter Meanwell and Lucy.*)

Meanwell

My dear Lucy! I can't conceive the meaning of your uncle's displeasure. His churlish behavior for some days past gives me great concern.

Lucy

He never uttered a syllable to your disadvantage 'till within these three days past, during which time he has been frequently dinning in my ears that if I marry agreeable to him, he'll give me ten thousand pounds to my portion, and further declared that if ever I spoke to you, or kept your company again, he'd disown me.

Meanwell

Strange! But pray, where's he to get the money?

Lucy

Oh, he's certainly beside himself or he couldn't entertain such notions. He told me last night he intended to sail for France the first opportunity, and there to get himself dubbed a Knight of the Golden Fleece.[41]

Meanwell

Unaccountable! Why, he must be out of his senses or he never could act so inconsistent; appoint tomorrow for the celebration of our nuptials, make the necessary preparation—then, all of a sudden, change his mind—I can't account for it.

Lucy

I hope his humor will shortly change—then we shall bring matters to a conclusion. For I had rather our marriage should be solemnized with than without, his consent.

Meanwell

Certainly it would be most agreeable to us both. But consent or not consent, it must be done.

Lucy

Our affair is carried too far for us to retract without subjecting us to the laughter of the town. You know, my dear Meanwell, a girl's character under these circumstances seldom escapes censure.

Meanwell

True, my dear Lucy. The world's very censorious, and slander, like a snowball, always gathers by rolling. Whatever malice can invent or envy suggest shall never lessen you in my esteem. My affection for you is too firm to be shaken by the blast of scandalous tongues.

Lucy

Be assured, your generous love shall be repaid with virtue, tenderness and respect. And if I had the ten thousand pounds my uncle shadowed out for me I should esteem it as so much dross—'twould only serve to make me miserable without you.
Air VII. "My Fond Shepherds, *etc.*"
(*Meanwell sings.*)

 My dear Lucy! You ravish my heart,
  I am blessed with such language as this;
 To my arms then—oh, come;—We'll never part,
  And let's mutually seal with a kiss.

(*Lucy sings.*)

 Ten thousand sweet kisses I'd give,
  Oh, be you contented with me,
 Then for you, my dear Meanwell, I'll live,
  And as happy as constant I'll be.

Lucy

Lord! Here's my uncle.
(*Enter Washball. Meanwell bows to him.*)

Washball

Hey dey! Here's fine doings! How dare you enter my house after I forbid you? Ha, sirrah?

Meanwell

Sir, your niece and—

Washball

—And what, sirrah, have you to do with my niece? Out of my house directly! You're a pretty fellow, indeed. Marry a girl with ten thousand pounds portion!

Meanwell

Sir, I beg—

Washball

Beg what? I'll have no beggars in my house, you rascal! Get out of my house, I say! What, do you want to rob me? Out of my house or I'll break your head, sirrah!

Lucy

Dear uncle! Be patient—

Washball

Patient, ha! What, you want him to stay, do you? Get to your room, you baggage! To your room this instant!
(*He attempts to strike her. Meanwell interposes and receives the blow.*)
Get out of the house, you villain! Away to your room, baggage! Out of my house, you rascal!
Exit Meanwell one way and Lucy another.)
If I ever find you here again, I'll send you to the workhouse, sirrah! Ten thousand pounds—ha!—To an upstart young fellow who hasn't so much as a coat of arms. Meanwell—I'm sure there's no such name to be found in all the books of heraldry. No, no, I'll match my niece to a nobleman who can trace his genealogy up as far as William the Conqueror, and can settle a good jointure on her.[42] I'll away to France, get myself created a Knight of the Golden Fleece. Then I shall have a greater coat-of-arms than any peer in Great Britain. I shall be called Sir John Washball, Knight of the Most Noble Order of the Golden Fleece—Oh, how I exult in the prospect! But I must away and meet my friends—the lucky hour approaches, when gold, diamonds and rubies shall make their appearance,
Which now lie dormant, in our mother earth,
But I must labor hard to give them birth.
(*Exit.*)

SCENE SEVEN: A Tavern.

(*Scene opens, and discovers Rattletrap, Hum, Parchment, Quadrant, McSnip, Raccoon, Trushoop and Washball seated around a table, drinking wine, etc.*)

Parchment

My old friend, Mr. Trushoop, how are you?

Trushoop

Oh hone'! My dear, at your sharwis. But I don't care how I am, so you are well.
(*Shakes hands.*)

Hum

Are we all here, gentlemen?

Quadrant

We're all here, Mr. Hum.

Hum

Well, gentlemen, things seem to go on prosperously, and bear a favorable aspect. I think myself happy in not having discovered this secret to any of the vain or profligate part of mankind, but to you, gentlemen, who by a long series of acquaintance I've found to be men of strict honor and integrity, and my very good friends. Which leaves me no room to doubt but the treasure we're about to discover and divide amongst us will be so disposed of as to render each of us useful members of society and shining ornaments to the government under which we live. It would grieve my heart to see any of us act contrary to the character of a man of piety, and a gentleman.

Trushoop

Arra, my dare, that's true for you! Don't you all hear that wery fine spache he made just now, a little while ago? By my shoul, he's a gentleman of great learnedness, fait', he is.

Raccoon

We t'ank broder Hum for his kind admonition. What he says is trute and seems to spring from de bery fountain of sense. And as my talent lies in de military, I intend to go to London and buy de regiment. Den I'll show dem what de Americans can do.
(*Rises and imitates the salute of the pike with his cane.*)
"Safe bind, safe find," eh, broder Hum? I had engaged with Mr. Trappick, and I have it under his own hand for a bill of exchange of t'ree thousand pounds, at sixty-five, at de rate of twenty-seven shilling de pistole and gold dust at six pound de ounce.[43]

Hum

It's very commendable, brother Raccoon. You have, to be sure, an excellent notion of honor and trade.

McSnip

In troth, I'se gang awa' and buy a teetle.

Washball

I am far advanced in years and have lost that sprightliness and activity I possessed in my youthful days, but I hope to do some good with my money. I propose to go over to France, get myself knighted, then to London and marry my niece to a nobleman. I've no ambition—not I—but to be called Sir John Washball and have a coat of arms.

Trushoop

The devil a hair do I care for a coat of arms, or a coat of legs. Myself will build a shapple and help the poor priests, who haven't a toot'ful to put in their mout's. And the devil a beggar shall l'ave my dure wid a hungry bally. And when I'm dead, shure they'll make a shaint o' me.

Parchment

I applaud your pious resolutions, Mr. Trushoop. Your intentional charity is certainly disinterested, and worthy of none but yourself.

Trushoop

The devil a word a lie in all that.

Rattletrap

Well, gentlemen, 'tis time to enter upon our business. Have you seriously considered what you are going about? Our warfare is not with men of this world—we have to engage with principalities and powers of darkness, with invisibles and demons far more powerful than the united legions of the most invincible monarchs on earth. Therefore, the greatest exertion of your courage will be necessary.

Trushoop

Fait', my dear, and you're right and I think so, too.

Parchment

The thought of these things shocks me so I can scarcely help trembling.

Raccoon

I t'ink I hab courage enough.

Hum

Aye, brother Raccoon, you're a happy man—your courage is constitutional.

Washball

Aye, so it is, so it is.—But as for me—oh dear!—oh dear!
(*McSnip sings.*)
Air VIII. "Over the Hills and Far Away."
   'Tis money makes the coward brave,
   And freedom gives to every slave;
   My gude broadsword I'll soon display,
   And drive these warlocks far away.
   And drive these warlocks, *etc.,*
   And drive these warlocks, *etc.,*
   My gude broadsword I'll soon display,
   And drive these warlocks far away.

Trushoop

By my showl! But I don't like the t'oughts of these dollughons.[44]

Raccoon

Come, don't be faint-heaterd, den. Put yourselbes under Mr. Rattletrap's care and mine.

Hum

We will so, brother Raccoon. It's happy for us we have you with us. Your example, no doubt, will inspire us with some degree of resolution.

Rattletrap

Well, are you all furnished with tools?

Raccoon

I've provided de pick-axe and de spade and de spit—I forgot to bring dem wid me. I left dem wid a friend, but I can hab dem for calling for.

Rattletrap

Now, gentlemen, let's fix on a watchword whereby we may know one another in the dark.
(*All say,* "By all means.")

Parchment
> The papers inform us that the treasure was carried up the creek on board a canoe.[45]

Washball
> A very good watchword, Mr. Parchment! Then let it be "canoe," as it has a reference to the concealment of the treasure.

Hum
> For my part, I like the word well.

McSnip
> Troth, I'se na' objection, sae we can understond ane another.

Trushoop
> The devil a hair myself cares how it is or what it is, canoe or boat, so we get the money.
> (*Sings.*)
> *Air IX.* "Chiling O' Guirey."
>> By Shaint Patrick, dear honeys, no longer let's stay,
>> But take l'ave all togather and bundle away,
>> To the plashe underground where the treasure's exposed,
>> And bring that to light which shall ne'er be disclosed.
>> And when we have got it, my jewels, Oh hone'!
>> For keeping it snug—arra!—let us alone.
>> We'll sing p'whillalew at the sight of the talf,[46]
>> And as for the sharing, l'ave that to myself.
>> Sing laral, lal, *etc.*
>>
>> II
>>
>> Arra! Feel how I'll work wid my pick-axe and spade,
>> For shure I was nursed to the turf-cutting trade,
>> In bright Tipperara and smiling Tyrone,
>> And if you'll all help me, we'll all dig alone.
>> Come, come then away, to the plashe we'll retrate,
>> If the devil should meet us he'll surely get bate.
>> I'll fasten my legs wid a pair of good brogues,
>> And I'll follow before all the way, my sweet rogues.
>> Sing laral, lal, *etc.*
>>
>> III
>>
>> And now we have got it, we'll roar and we'll bawl,
>> And sing, fait', like locusts in winter or fall.
>> With shamrock in hat, de'el a down will we lay,

But dance all night long on Saint Patrick's Day;
The bagpipes shall fiddle "Gramudgey Gramaugh,"[47]
While we swill down skolrankey or good usquebaugh.[48]
When I walk in the strate I'll be led by a troop
Coming after, long life to dear ma'aster Trushoop.
Sing laral, lal, *etc.*

Rattletrap

Well, gentlemen, at eleven o'clock we're to meet at the stone bridge.[49] It will not be prudent to go all together, lest we be discovered. Whoever arrives there first, let him wait for the rest, and as they come up, hail them with the word "canoe." They must answer with the same word. By observing this we shall prevent all discovery.

Hum

Aye, aye, the utmost care and circumspection are necessary—we can't be too cautious.

Trushoop

Fait', and I'll holler "canoe" and "canoe" all night long 'till daylight, if you pl'ase.

Rattletrap

Except you are determined to follow my directions when we come to action, 'twill be in vain to proceed.

Washball

The spirits won't hurt us, I hope.

Rattletrap

Take no rash steps, don't be afraid, follow my directions and not a hair on your heads shall be injured.

Washball

I'll do nothing but what you order, Mr. Rattletrap.

Trushoop

You're right, my dare, and by my shoul, so will I, and more, too!

Rattletrap

'Tis needless to say any more. Remember, eleven o'clock at the stone bridge. Each of you repair home and bring your tools with you. Be punctual at the hour. We break up for the present. I'll

away home and put on my magic habit—otherwise, I shall have no
power over the invisibles.

Raccoon

I'll go and get de tools, and I'll bring a little refreshment wid me.

Trushoop

Fait', and I'll bring my gauging rod and all the tools in the shop
if you want them.[50] Because why?—I'll have no occasion to use
them after this.

McSnip

I'se feetch me andra wi' me, and then I'se feece the de'el himsel',
'gin he appears.[51]

Quadrant

I'll bring the instruments—they're all in good order and well prepared.

Rattletrap

Now, gentlemen, let's go with good hearts. There's nothing like
putting a good face on these matters—if you'll bear a chorus, I'll
sing you a song before we set off. Come, fill your glasses.
(*All say,* "With all our hearts." *They fill their glasses.*)
(*Rattletrap sings.*)
Air X. "The Jolly Toper."
            The merchant roams from clime to climes.
                  Regardless of his pleasure;
            To hardships and fatigue resigns,
                  When in pursuit of treasure.
            And a digging, *etc.*
(*They drink and fill.*)
                                 II
            See, now the lucky hour it comes,
                  With pick-axe and with spade;
            A little digging, oh, my sons!
                  And then our fortune's made.
            And a digging, *etc.*
(*Drink and fill.*)
                                 III
            Let's boldly venture on the ground,
                  And seize the glorious chest;

No joy on earth like gold is found,
  To ease the human breast.
And a digging, *etc.*
(*All drink, huzza and exeunt.*)

END OF THE FIRST ACT.

ACT TWO.

SCENE ONE: A Room in
Moll Placket's House.

(*Enter Topinlift and Moll Placket.*)

Topinlift

What cheer, Moll? Let's taste your head!
(*Kisses her.*)
How stands the wind?[52] Is the coast clear? No danger of the
enemy?

Placket

No, no, we're safe enough for three or four hours. He has no
certain time of coming, except after church on Sundays, and then
he never fails. If the old fellow succeeds in this night's enterprise
I'll make your fortune for you, my boy.

Topinlift

Why, what the devil's Raccoon spied now? Is there a galleon in
chase, or is he going to turn pirate?

Placket

No, no, but he may thank the pirates for it.

Topinlift

How? How, Moll? Tell me, you little dear dog, you.

Placket

Tell you, indeed!—Well, can you keep a secret?

Topinlift

If ever I blow you, blast me! You know me better—if one word
goes through my head-rails, the devil blow me to jillkicker! Aye,
Moll, the next hurricane blow me off the mainyard, three leagues
astern. That's enough—and now I'll kiss the book on it.[53]
(*Kisses her.*)

Placket

Well, then, I'll tell you—you must know that Mr. Hum has received a letter from his sister in England, giving an account where
there's a great deal of money that was buried by the pirates.

Topinlift

Money buried by the pirates? The devil! I've often heard that Blackbeard hid his money near the riverside somewhere—but how the devil came she by these papers?

Placket

Why, she's Captain Blackbeard's granddaughter—the papers were preserved in the family 'till they were sent to Mr. Hum. And you must know that Raccoon is a freemason, so he is to assist him and they are to go shares.

Topinlift

How the devil do you know that Hum's a freemason?

Placket

Why, I suppose so, for they always call one another "brother," and they keep this business as secret as their masonry. But I wheedled him out of it, in spite of all their cunning.

Topinlift

I shouldn't like him on board the *Europa*—he'd made a damned fist in the Killecranky trade.[54] He'd throw out a signal and the custom-house officers would soon bear down on us—away goes ship and cargo by the mast! He'd soon make my owners scratch a beggar's arse. But tell us, Moll, how the devil did you pump it out of him?

Placket

That's none of your business, sauce-box. Women like me have always a lure to catch the men's secrets.

Topinlift

True, Moll. But this sort of chit-chat keeps us at long-shot—I thought to have grappled with you by this time.[55] Let's step into the state-room and turn in. You know the old saying—time and tide wait for no one.

Placket

Softly—don't be too hasty—let's make the door fast first.
(*She locks the door.*)[56]
Though I love your little finger better than Raccoon's whole body, yet I must keep in with him.

Topinlift

Aye, that's true, Moll. I should be loath to quarrel with an owner because he didn't understand navigation.

Placket

You know he maintains me, finds me a house to live in, fathers all my children—And a husband can do no more.

Topinlift

Right, Moll. Now we're all snug—the hatches are all secured. (*Sings.*)
Air XI. "Nancy Dawson."

No girl with Placket can compare,
She is so charming, sweet and fair,
Her rosy cheeks and nut-brown hair,
There's none like Molly Placket.
Whene'er from sea I do return,
For my dear Placket how I burn;
Good luck, Raccoon! 'Tis now my turn;
Come, come, my lovely Placket.
Chorus, *etc.*

Come, Moll, now I'll try what the clews of your hammock are made of.[57]
(*As they walk towards the upper part of the stage a scene opens, and discovers a bed, table, and two bottles on it, with a broken glass over one of them and a candle stuck in the other.*)
(*A knocking at the door.*)
So—the devil has owed me a spite this good while, and now he's brought the enemy upon me when I'm landlocked.

Placket

Who's there? Who's there?

Raccoon

(*Without.*)
It's me, my dear little pet. Open the door.

Placket

Oh, curse his head! Pet's a'coming, dear Coony, pet's a'coming.

Topinlift

Where the devil shall I stow myself? Show me where to hide!

Placket

Creep under the bed and you're as safe as a thief in a mill.
(*Topinlift goes under the bed. She opens the door.*)
(*Enter Raccoon.*)

Placket

What brings my dear Coony back so soon? No misfortune, I hope.

Raccoon

No, no, no misfortune, my dear pet—only I left some t'ings under
de bed.

Placket

(*Aside.*)
Curse your contrivance! Now I'm blown!
(*To Raccoon.*)
What things, my dear Coony, did you leave here?
(*Aside.*)
Oh invention, thou darling genius of my sex! Assist me, or I'm
ruined!

Raccoon

Not'ing, my dear pet, but de spade, de pick-axe and de spit—But
what makes you look so surprised, my child?

Placket

Why, I was afraid you'd catch me—
(*Affects a laugh.*)
—and indeed you'd like to have done it. Ha, ha, ha!

Raccoon

Ketch what? Ketch how? What de devil do you mean by "ketch"?
Egad, I begin to t'ink it isn't all lies I hear of you, Mrs. Placket.
Tell me instantly who you had wid you, or I'll shake you to atoms!
(*He shakes her and she bawls.*)
What de devil do you t'ink to impose on me with your hee, hee,
hee's? I'll know de trute before I done, hussy!

Placket

Oh, my dear Coony! Do let me go and I'll tell you the truth.

Topinlift

(*Peeping from under the bed.*)
Oh, the brimstone whore! I wish I was on board the *Europa!*

Raccoon
   Well, come, let's hear—confine yourself to de trute, hussy.

Topinlift
   (*Peeping.*)
   By the Lord, the storm gathers! We shall have foul weather soon
   —I must bowse taut my rolling tackles.[58]

Placket
   La, sir, I'm afraid to tell you, you're so angry. I'll tell you in the
   morning, when your passion's over.

Raccoon
   I'll know it instantly, you vile strumpet! Or I'll—
   (*Shakes her again and she bawls.*)

Topinlift
   (*Peeping.*)
   It comes thicker and faster—here's a damned stink of bilgewater
   alongside.

Placket
   I'll tell! I'll tell you all if you won't hurt me.

Raccoon
   Well, tell den.

Placket
   Look at this book.
   (*Gives him a Dutch almanac.*)

Raccoon
   Dis book? What of dat? It's High-Dutch.

Placket
   Can't you read it?

Raccoon
   Not I, indeed.

Placket
   (*Aside.*)
   I'm glad of it.
   (*To Raccoon.*)
   Why then you must know when I was about fifteen years of age I
   lived with my uncle at Germantown—a High-German doctor who

could tell fortunes, detect lost maidenheads, lay spirits, raise the devil, find stolen goods and discover hidden treasure. And all his whole art is contained in this little book.[59]

Raccoon

Well, what's all dat to de purpose?

Placket

Nothing, but I'd just taken the book in my hand and was about to raise a familiar spirit to inform me if you'd succeed in your undertaking, and he was just rising through the floor when you knocked at the door.

Raccoon

(*Starts, changes his tone, and trembles.*)
I declare you surprise me—let me get the t'ings and I'll go.

Placket

No! No, 'tis as much as your life's worth to touch anything before I've drove him off.

Topinlift

(*Peeping.*)
By my soul, she acts her part well! She'd out-face truth and out-brazen the devil! A girl after my own heart, faith.

Raccoon

Can you lay him den, pet?

Placket

Why, I've raised and laid five hundred in my time—don't be afraid.

Topinlift

(*Peeping.*)
That's true for you, my girl—I'll swear for fifty. But I'll secure the spit for fear of the worst.

Placket

Would you like to see him?

Raccoon

No! No—ah—ah—dere's no 'casion.
(*She places his back toward the bed.*)

Placket

Well, stand here—don't stir an inch! Bend your head a little that way, and keep your eyes shut. He's visible—but don't be afraid.

Raccoon

(*Trembling.*)
Oh—oh—I wish he was gone!

Placket

(*Beckons to Topinlift: he comes from under the bed, she meets him and puts an old petticoat over his head and shoulders. She reads:*)
Dunder schlemer hoont, shize-treek, un calevreva, rizum, tenealis amisce![60]
(*Topinlift runs, oversets old Raccoon, drops the spit and runs off.*)

Raccoon

(*Looking frightened.*)
Mercy on me! Bere am I?

Placket

Get up, my dear! Did you see it? You ain't hurt, I hope, my dear. Let me help you up.
(*She takes hold of him.*)
Don't be frightened, he's gone far enough now—he'll not trouble you any more.
(*She applies a smelling bottle to his nose, he starts and smells.*)

Raccoon

Oh, my dear! I neber was so frightened in all my life! Is he gone?

Placket

Didn't you see him?

Raccoon

I had de glimp' of him as he goed by. I t'ought he had—ah—ah— carried de corner of de house away wid him.

Placket

(*Runs to the bottle and brings a dram to him.*)
Will you have a dram, my dear Coony? Here, drink it, my dear, and you'll recover your spirits.

Raccoon

(*Trembling, drinks.*)
Oh, I wasn't a-a-afraid, my dear, o-o-only—

Placket

>Courage, man! Come, rise.
>(*She helps him up.*)
>You'll see ten times more before morning.

Raccoon

>Oh, I'm not afraid. I seed him—I t'ink he look like de sailor.

Placket

>Why, he's the apparition of one of Captain Blackbeard's crew, and
>as a confirmation that you'll obtain the treasure he threw that spit
>on the floor as he flew off.

Raccoon

>Why, dis is de bery spit dat I put under de bed.

Placket

>If so you must lose no time, but begone.

Raccoon

>Well, I'll get de pick-axe and de spade, and den I'll go.
>(*He goes to the bed and takes them.*)
>Now, one buss, my dear pet, and den—
>(*Sings.*)
>*Air XII.* "The Lass of Patie's Mill."
>>Oh, when I get de we'lt' dat's buried by de mill,
>>Insured long life and he'lt', and pleasure at my will.
>>What store of gold I'll bring, my lovely pet, to dee,
>>Den none but my poor t'ing shall share the same wid me.
>(*Exit.*)

Placket

>Well, it's an old saying, "when poverty comes in at the door, love
>flies out of the window." Really, I've experienced the truth of it
>lately! Hadn't it been for Topinlift and a few transient friends, I
>believe I should have been in a poor situation by this time—for
>I'm sure he's nothing about him that can please me but his money.
>He promises what he will do—this thing, and the other thing—but
>I'll no longer trust to bare promises. He has deceived me long
>enough! I should have been better off if I had never seen his face.
>Yet, had he dealt honorably by me I should have done the same
>by him. But when a woman finds herself deceived, basely treated,
>abused and deprived of real necessaries, she has it always in her

power—and she must be a fool if she don't take her revenge in a way most pleasing to herself.[61]

(*Sings.*)

Air XIII. "Black-joke and Band So White."

    Sure gold is the jewel that kindles the fire,
    And serves for to fan up a woman's desire,
        To a fumbling fool that's decrepid and old.
    For in all scenes of life from the great to the little,
    The bench, bar, and pulpit, it suits to a tittle.
        You're surely condemned if you haven't the gold,
    But if you have money, ne'er mind what your cause is,
    But tickle their palms and you'll gain their applauses.
    No statesman so great, so cunning and bold,
    But will truckle to you for the sake of your gold.
    But if you lack that, you are certainly sold.
        But hang this disappointment! Then—
    Let women of business take care of their men,
    If one won't suffice them, why let them have ten!

(*Exit.*)

SCENE TWO: The Place of Action,
near the Stone Bridge.

(*Scene opens and discovers Rattletrap, dressed in his magic habit, with a dark lantern and candle: Spitfire with a dark lantern and candle: Quadrant with a magnet, rod and wand, a chest and a figure representing the head and shoulders of Blackbeard.*)

Rattletrap

Well, that's right—the holes, I see, are made.

Spitfire

Yes, I've not been idle since you left me.

Quadrant

We must lose no time—'tis near eleven o'clock.
(*They poke in the chest two or three rusty pieces of silver.*)
Come, come bury it at once.
(*They all assist and bury the chest.*)

Rattletrap

> (*To Spitfire.*)
> Now we've nothing more to do than to see you safe in your hole.[62]
> Step down, step down, and mind—when I give you the signal,
> throw fireballs. And when they come to a sight of the chest, push
> up the figure. Now be sure you act the devil as if you were going to
> deceive the devil himself, and we'll reward you devilishly well.

Spitfire

> And the devil take me if I don't.
> (*Spitfire goes down the hole and takes the figure and the lantern
> and candle with him.*)

Quadrant

> Now I think we're right. We're ready to receive them, and if our
> devil plays his part well I think we shall make a devilish merry
> night of it. Ha, ha, ha! Egad, here's some of them.
> (*He halloos.*)
> Canoe!
> (*They answer without,* "canoe, canoe.")
> (*Enter Hum and Parchment,* hallooing "canoe.")

Rattletrap

> Where are the rest of you?

Parchment

> They're all coming. I heard them as we came down the hill.
> (*Different voices without, hallooing,* "canoe." *One after another,
> they on the stage answering them with the same word.*)
> (*Enter Washball, Trushoop, McSnip and Raccoon, with pick-axe,
> spades and spit shouldered.*)

Washball

> I tore my shins unaccountably, coming through the briars.

Trushoop

> Fait', and I tumbled up the hill 'till I got my fut in the bogs. And
> if I hadn't held fast by the water I'd be drowned.

Raccoon

> Don't mind, gentlemen. What is de broken shin or de cold foot,
> compared wid the prospect of dese riches?

McSnip

By my saul! I charged my sel' wi' twa bottles to lengthen me nawse
—and that's a bonny good in a dark neet.[63] And for fear of meeting wi' any scoondrils, I'se brought my andra under my co't—as
gude stuff as e'er was made in aw' Scotland.

Rattletrap

Well, gentlemen—are we all here?
(*He calls them over by their name.*)
(*All say,* "We're here, Mr. Rattletrap.")

Rattletrap

Keep silence, gentlemen! By the calculation I made this morning,
by the Satellites, it must be somewhere near this place.[64]
(*He sets his magnet.*)

Raccoon

Dis seems a likely place, broder Hum. Now let us hab a good
heart.

Hum

Let me beg of you, brother Raccoon, not to be too fierce.
I am fearful your courage will get the better of your prudence.

Rattletrap

Not a word! Not a word, gentlemen! The magnet works this way—
pray be silent! Where's my rod?
(*Quadrant gives him the rod, and he works it.*)
It draw excessive strong this way. I can feel myself interrupted by
invisibles—I can scarcely keep the rod in my hands! There! Now
I have it. It draws this way!

Raccoon

Dis is de critical moment, gentlemen! Now, gentlemen!

Hum

You've too much courage, brother Raccoon. Pray be advised.

Rattletrap

Silence! I'm near the place! The rod points to this spot. I'm near
the center! I know the rod to be good—I've tried its virtue. 'Twas
cut on All-Hallow's Eve, at twelve o'clock at night, with my back
to the moon, and the mercury injected while the sap was running.[65]

Trushoop

By the Holy Stone! I believe he was born in the moon!

Rattletrap

Not a word, gentlemen!
(*He draws a circle with his wand, and speaks these words:*)
Diapaculum interravo, testiculum stravaganza.[66]

Trushoop

By my showl, my dear! And he speaks halgebra to it!

Washball

Oh dear! Oh dear! You'll spoil all!
(*Rattletrap goes round the circle and sticks twelve pieces of iron wire in the periphery; each wire having a piece of paper cut out in form of a star on its head. As he sticks them into the ground he names the twelve signs of the zodiac.*)

Rattletrap

Aries, Taurus, Gemini, Cancer, Leo, Virgo, Libra, Scorpio, Sagittarius, Capricornus, Aquarius, Pisces. Make no motion else you'll disturb Jupiter, who is the most wakeful planet. He is now in his first sleep.
(*He puts on a large pair of spectacles.*)
Let me see—it's now twelve o'clock. The moon is nearing her southing; Jupiter is in a sound sleep. A good omen.

Raccoon

(*To Hum.*)
What does he say—'Upiter? Is 'Upiter a lucky omen, broder Hum?

Hum

Don't speak! Don't speak, good brother Raccoon, pray don't! Let me entreat you!

Rattletrap

(*Calls Washball, Trushoop, McSnip, and Raccoon.*) Take off your clothes, gentlemen.
(*They pull off their coats and jackets.*)
And stand within this circle.
(*He places Hum, Quadrant, and Parchment without the circle at different posts and says:*)

Keep a good lookout—"canoe's" the word, don't forget it! Now, run down the spit and try this place, Mr. Washball.

Washball

(*Thrusts down the spit and cries out.*)
I feel it! I feel it! It strikes against something!

Rattletrap

Then fall to and dig! And when the signal's given, fall flat on your faces!
(*They dig.*)
Now the Dragon's head and Scorpion's tail are in conjunction—a lucky concurrence. But Sagittarius seems eclipsed. Ha! I don't like that—it looks portentous of ill. But Syrius's right foot—

Parchment

Canoe!
(*They all answer "canoe!" and fall down within the circle.*)

Rattletrap

Inferno atum, gastro phagnum! Rise up and go on—it was only a blind fiddler and some company returning from the Bachelor's Hall.[67]
(*They rise and dig.*)

Trushoop

By my showl, but I've made a swate pickle of myself, all over full of mud.

McSnip

De'el tauk me, mon, but I dinna' leeke this.

Rattletrap

Not a word—proceed! But Syrius's right foot over Orion's left shoulder looks well. And the Swan's tail near the Hydra's heart looks well, too.
(*One fireball, with a roaring below. The diggers frightened, and attempt to run out of the circle.*)
Don't stir an inch! If you do break the bounds, I've no power! Dig! Dig! *Conjabetima morentium habavo!* And this leap year is not unfavorable.
(*Another fireball, with a roaring below, at which the diggers seem terrified.*)

Trushoop

Oh, how my heart bates!

Washball

Come nearer to me, Mr. Rattletrap, or I shall faint! Oh dear! Oh dear!

Raccoon

Oh, oh, I wish I was at home; I neber would come again.

Rattletrap

Never fear—I'll protect you. *Hobonos cum verigos, omne croxibus influvientum.*

Hum

Canoe!

(*All answer* "canoe" *and fall down.*)

Rattletrap

Mentantaborabulum exultisimo, locabulus mongrabo! Rise, 'twas nothing but a cow.

(*They all rise and dig.*)

Trushoop

Arra, how my wife will scowld at me when I fetch her the money, for spoiling my new coat.

Rattletrap

Sagittarius is clear. Sextile in conjunction with Quartile—right!

(*He waves his wand.*)

Saturn is a metallic planet, and though in common the most dull, he looks clearer than the rest. This is the best sign of all.

(*Another fireball with a roaring below.*)

Washball

Oh dear! Oh dear! Speak to it, Mr. Rattletrap.

Rattletrap

These invisibles will disturb you a while—you're just upon it. *Conjunction oppositorium, placabulum fomoso!* Dig away! Arcturus now appears—Venus is now our morning star and is eclipsed four digits.

(*Two or three fireballs and a roaring.*)

Now their rage increases! We're nigh the treasure—don't be afraid

—keep up your spirits—I am with you—their fiery darts will soon be over.

Hum

    (*Aside.*)

    He performs to perfection.

Quadrant

    (*Aside.*)

    Incomparably well, by Jupiter! Ha, ha, ha!

    (*Three or four fireballs and an increase of roaring.*)

Rattletrap

    Cum meritantibus considerationibus, terrabandum ophagnum.

Parchment

    (*Aside.*)

    See how that goose gobbles down the Latin as a duck would a chitterlin.

Washball

    Mercy on us! Mercy on us! I shall faint.

Rattletrap

    Don't be frightened—now Cassiopeia and the Bear's Tail are on the meridian. Excessive lucky!

Quadrant

    (*Aside.*)

    Come, let's drink while the fools are digging. Ha, ha, ha!

    (*They drink and keep pointing and laughing at the diggers.*)

McSnip

    It's confoonded hard work—it makes me swete.

Raccoon

    I feel de chest! I feel de chest!

    (*The ghost appears, spits fire. The diggers, with upraised hands, look at it.*)

Trushoop

    By my showl, but I've a great mind to wauk off wid myself, for the devil burn me but I believe he'll burn us all up! For—fait'!—he looks like no slouch of a fellow.

McSnip

    Troth, mon, he c'uts a shacking figure.

Washball

    (*With upturned hands, kneeling, sings:*)
    Mea culpa, mea culpa, mea maxima culpa!

Raccoon

    Pray in English, dese pirate spirits don't understand de Latin!
    (*He kneels, lifts up his hands, and says:*)
    I don't know what to say. I wish I had lib'd a better life. Dear Mr.
    Washball, say you' prayers.

Washball

    I can't pray in English—do you say something good to it!

Rattletrap

    Cruciblarium, adventum perilorum!
    (*The ghost disappears, they rise and tremble with fear. The ghost
    appears again and spits fire: all fall on their knees.*)

Raccoon

    Right worshipful master—oh—oh! I believe—ah—ah—What is
    your name? Raccoon. Who gib you dat name? My grandmoders
    and godfaders. Oh, oh, oh, for eber and eber, amen. Dare he
    comes! Dare he comes again!

Trushoop

    (*To Raccoon.*)
    L'ave off you' black mout'! You haven't it—let's have no more of
    that!
    (*He sings.*)
    Sinnerorum helpum deliverum, miserabulum tuscarorum.

McSnip

    By my saul, mon, 'tis the de'el himsel'!

Washball

    Save me! Save me!

Rattletrap

    (*To the ghost.*)
    Superiorum lakehavi, hurorum.
    (*The ghost disappears.*)

Now's the lucky minute—the Serpent's neck is round the pole-aster.[68] Raise the chest.

(*They rise and raise the chest; the ghost appears and spits fire. A great roaring below. The diggers all shriek and tremble; Hum, Quadrant, and Parchment laughing at them aside.*)

Rattletrap

Now gentlemen, keep your hold—banish fear—keep fast!

(*He calls to Hum, Quadrant, and Parchment.*)

Your assistance, gentlemen, or we shall lose all.

(*They run to them and assist in raising the chest.*)

Raccoon

(*Looking toward the ghost, says:*)

Dat's old Blackbeard! By de birtue and de power of de free and de accepted mason, to me giben, I command you to depa't! Oh, oh, oh, what distu'bs dy poor soul from rest?

McSnip

Hold fast—do na' let gang your grup.

(*He looks toward the ghost.*)

Now I ken him, I'll gang after him.

Raccoon

Pray don't, Mr. McSnip, it's de pirate apparition. Didn't you see how bery angry it looked at me when I did speak to it?

McSnip

I do na' care what it is! Be it sperit, appareetion, or the de'el him-sel', I'se try my bro'd-sword on him. 'Gin he can stond a cut o' my andra, he mun be the de'el in troth.

(*He takes up the broadsword, runs after it, makes a cut at it and falls down. The ghost disappears for a short time, returns again, spitting fire, the roaring continuing below. McSnip lies on the ground and says:*)

De'el tak' aw warlocks, I say—I had leken to ha' brok' me neck down the brae.

Rattletrap

That was a very wrong step. If I hadn't been here you would have suffered by your impetuosity.

(*He steps up to the ghost and says:*)

Horridum, callifridum, buscantivo, interdenabulum—Avaunt!

Avaunt! Avaunt! And be thou laid in Lake Huron while water flows![69]

(*The ghost disappears.*)

Now we're all safe. Up with the chest—these fiends of darkness will trouble us no more.

(*They hoist up the chest and turn it over. Some rusty-looking pieces of silver tumble out.*)

McSnip

(*Rises up, shakes himself and says:*)

The de'el a sight more you'll ha' o' him, now he's gotten a smell o' my andra.

(*All:* Huzza! huzza! huzza! *etc.*)

Washball

(*Greedily taking up one of the pieces of silver, kisses it and says:*)

Oh my dear, my dear!

(*He rubs it, takes it to the lantern and says:*)

Let me see . . . 1634. Aye, this is the very money that Blackbeard got at Panama when he robbed the churches.[70] Oh, the poor priests! The poor priests! It seems providentially to have fallen into my hands. Come, come, let us take it away.

Hum

May we presume to take it away, Mr. Rattletrap?

Rattletrap

My business is finished, therefore all is our own.

Hum

There's one thing, gentlemen, proper to mention—my sister from whom we've received this information is entitled to a share. Besides, I think she merits a handsome present from us.

Raccoon

Yes, broder Hum, I t'ink she's entitled to one share—but what present do you talk of?

Hum

Why, I shall leave that to you, gentlemen. What think you of a couple o' thousand pistoles, or some such trifle?

Raccoon

Consider, gentlemen, we had run de risk of our libes wid dese spirits. Beside, dat's a great deal too much.

Hum
> Suppose it should be a service of plate of that value? Put it to vote.

Raccoon
> I t'ink it's a bery great shame.
> (*The others say*, "plate, plate, plate.")

Hum
> Well, gentlemen, I'm satisfied.

Rattletrap
> The day approaches—remove it immediately.

Parchment
> Where shall we carry it?

Washball
> There's room in my house—I'll take care of it. It shall be safe—
> I'll sleep on it all night.
> (*All say*, "Agreed, agreed, agreed.")

Hum
> Gentlemen, let's all meet presently at eight o'clock and divide the
> money. I think it's necessary some of us should assist Mr. Wash-
> ball—as this chest contains an immense treasure, we can't be too
> careful. He's aged, and some accident may happen.

Raccoon
> I t'ink I'd better go too, as I understand de military. If we should
> be attacked, my service may be necessary.

Parchment
> You're right, sir, and if Mr. McSnip and Mr. Trushoop will at-
> tend you, it will be the safer.

Trushoop
> The devil burn Trushoop if he forsakes 'em.

McSnip
> De'el tauk the mon that lags beheend.

Rattletrap
> Well, gentlemen, I think this great success deserves a song. Come,
> bear a chorus.
> (*All say*, "With all our hearts.")
> *Air XIV*. "Granby."

I

Though my art some despise, I appeal to your eyes,
    For a proof of my magical knowledge;
Though the wisdom of schools damn our art and our tools,
    We can laugh at the fools of the college.
(Chorus.)

II

Now my friends, we're possessed of the glorious chest,
    Join hands and rejoice beyond measure:
Let it be our first care that great blessing to share,
    Whose contents are an infinite treasure.
(Chorus.)
(*The dupes take up the chest and bear it off, guarded by the humorists. Going off they say:*)

Washball

It feels brave and ponderous.

Trushoop

It is so, my dare, but fait'! I don't care if I broke my back wid it—arra, dare! Tr'ad off my hales.

McSnip

I beg your pardon, mon.

Trushoop

Fait', my dare, and you're wery welcome. For the devil burn me if I'm thinking about my hales at all, at all.
(*Exeunt.*)

SCENE THREE: A Room
in Washball's House.

(*Enter Meanwell [and Lucy].*)

Lucy

Bless me! How could you venture, after the severe reproof my uncle gave you, to approach this house at this dead time of night?

Meanwell

Love! Angelic love, which knows no fear but your displeasure, has brought me here on angel's wings to waft you hence, and seal that vow already ratified in heaven.

Lucy

But consider, my dear Meanwell, what may be the consequence of such a rash step, when perhaps a few days' perseverance may bring matters to a conclusion with his consent?

Meanwell

I cannot think of trusting to anything so precarious. As he has already consented by being my bondsman for the license, and publicly declaring his assent, we shall be looked upon by the honest and judicious as sufficiently justified in taking this step.

Lucy

I am confounded! My love to you spurs me to flight, but my duty to my uncle commands me to wait his reconciliation. I know not what to do or what to say.

Meanwell

Haste! Haste, my dear Lucy! We've no time to lose! Each moment seems an hour 'till we're one! The clergyman waits with chosen friends to tie the nuptial knot, and crown our bliss.

Air XV. "Kitty, the Nonpareile."

(*Lucy sings.*)

My throbbing heart must now give way,
To love, to honor and obey,
   Lo! Hymen's torch is lighted. Lo! Hymen's torch, *etc.*
My heart, my all, I do resign,
Oh! Meanwell, Meanwell, I'll be thine,
   In wedlock's bands united. In wedlock's, *etc.*

(*Meanwell sings.*)

Of Venus's charms let poets write,
Diana chaste, or Juno bright,
   Of Kitty, Doll, or Susy: Of Kitty, *etc.*
The charms of all are centered here,
In Lucy, charming Lucy dear!
   Haste, haste, my lovely Lucy! Haste, *etc.*

(*Exeunt.*)

SCENE FOUR: A Street.

(*Enter Washball.*)

Washball

I can't bear the thought of dividing, not I. Division—why, I could

never learn it at school! One hundred thousand pounds, divided
into nine parts—let me see . . . three times nine is . . . ah . . .
ah . . . eighty-nine! That's wrong—nine times eleven is a hundred
and six and four over—that's too much. But I'm no scholar. Well,
never mind, no matter—charity begins at home, and he must be
the greatest fool on earth that cheats himself—the sin will lie at
his own door and it will be out of his power to make restitution.
I'll go and inform the Collector, then I shall have one-half to myself, the other will go to the king.[71] They'll call me traitor, but I
don't care. Let them laugh that wins. It's an old saying, and a
true one—that is—let me see . . . aye, I have it! One bird in hand
is better far than two that's in the bush—no, no, than two that in
the bushes are.[72] Aye, that's it! I remember it's so on my neighbor
Symond's sign. But here's fifty thousand birds in the cage, and all
pretty yellow-birds every one of them—oh, they'll make delightful
music and make me sing, too—I'll e'en go to the Collector—I
mustn't lose any time—no, no. (*He looks up.*) I think this is the
house—aye. (*He knocks at the door, the Collector appears.*)

Collector

What is your business, sir?

Washball

Why—why, sir, I have an information to make you concerning a
chest of treasure that was dug out of the ground last night. Mr.
Hum, sir, and several others are concerned, and it grieves my conscience to cheat the king of his lawful right. So, pray, sir, seize it
immediately, for me and his majesty. I expect all concerned will be
at my house immediately to open and share it. Put the broad R on
it and then we shall be safe.[73] You must act for me and the king,
and we'll reward you handsomely.

Collector

Pooh, 'tis not possible—it's only some scheme to make you ridicu-
lous.

Washball

Indeed, sir, it's a real truth—for this piece of money—
(*Showing the piece.*)
—dropped out of the chest when we took it out of the ground.
Look here, sir, see it. Pray be expeditious! Do, sir, be expeditious!

Collector
> Well, sir, if you insist on it, I must seize it.

Washball
> My loyalty to the king obliges me to insist on it.

Collector
> I'll wait on you.
> (*Exeunt.*)

SCENE FIVE: A Room in Washball's House.

(*Scene opens and discovers McSnip, Trushoop and Raccoon sitting on the chest, and old Gabriel, Washball's servant, standing by.*)

(*Enter Hum, Parchment, Quadrant, and Rattletrap.*)

Parchment
> Gabriel! Where's your master?

Gabriel
> He's just stepped out, sir.

Hum
> Will he be in soon?

Gabriel
> Aye, I believe he will.

Quadrant
> Oh, here he comes—but who the devil's that with him?

Parchment
> The Collector! Egad, this is what I did not expect!
> (*Aside to Hum.*)
> It will not do to dupe him—we must let him into the secret.

Hum
> (*To Parchment.*)
> Leave that to me.
> (*Enter Collector and Washball. Hum takes the Collector aside and says:*)
> Sir, I am sorry we have been the means of giving you this trouble—it's a scheme of diversion only—please not to notice it.

Collector

(*Aside.*)

Just as I thought! Mr. Hum, your servant. Gentlemen, yours.

Washball

Sir, sir, I beg you stay! Pray do your duty.

Collector

Mr. Washball, it's an affair too intricate for me. I must first advise with the king's attorney.

(*Exit.*)

Trushoop

Augh! You cursed old traitor! Aren't you ashamed of yoursalf to be cheating us after this way?

Quadrant

I never heard of such a villain!

Gabriel

(*Aside.*)

Here's queer doings here.

McSnip

Ye eenfamous auld scoondril! Ye turned eenformer to get the ane half to yoursel'! But ye're oot, mon! I'se a mind to leeghten your heed by ane o' your luggs.

Gabriel

(*Aside.*)

Worse and worse.

Raccoon

What did you t'ink—we were all fools to be cheated by you?

Hum

Nothing can equal this! Open the chest, gentlemen—who knows but the king's attorney will be upon our backs directly.

Parchment

A traitor, gentlemen, of all mankind is the most despicable wretch. You see, gentlemen, that old curmudgeon thinks nothing of betraying his soul for the sake of his body. Not the least regard to his solemn oath!

Gabriel

(*Aside.*)

How he abuses my master!

Quadrant

Mr. Trushoop, where's your adze? Open the chest.

Trushoop

Augh, fait', and here we are bot', at your sarviss, my dare.

Washball

(*Strives to prevent them: Hum, Rattletrap, Parchment, and Quadrant hold him, he struggles to get from them and bawls:*)

Where's the Collector? Mr. Collector! Touch it at your peril, you villains! I'll swear robbery against you!

Gabriel

(*Aside.*)

I believe they're going to rob my master.

Parchment

Go on with your business, gentlemen, open the chest.

(*Trushoop, Raccoon and McSnip open the chest.*)

Washball

Touch it at your peril, I say! It belongs to me and the king!

Trushoop

Belong to the devil, you t'ief! We'll soon see who'll feel the sharing of it!

Gabriel

(*Lifting up his hands.*)

I never see the like before.

Washball

Murder! Murder! Fire! Thieves! Ravishment! Hell and fury! Betty! Betty, bring down the bags you made! Run, Gabriel, and call the Collector!

Gabriel

Yes, I will, and I'll go for the constable. Sorrow on me but I believe they'll murder my master.

(*Exit.*)

Raccoon

Dere! De chest opens.

McSnip

It's aupen.

(*They let Washball go; he runs toward the chest; the dupes all scramble to get their shares, and in the scuffle push down Washball and overset the chest; out tumble the contents.*)

Washball

(*Rising.*)

Give me my share! Give me my share! Give me my share!

(*McSnip, Trushoop, Raccoon and Washball look at one another confused.*)

McSnip

Hoot mon! What the de'el's aw this? Nathing but staines[74]—I ken weel enough wha' it is—de'el dem me first, but I'll ha' jontlemen's saytisfakeshon.

Trushoop

Fait', and we're all humbugged.

Raccoon

De devil! Dis is a scheme of broder Hum's—I'll second your resolution, Mr. McSnip—do you gib de challenge.

Trushoop

By my showl, and I've been made a fool of for the future! But I'll take care for the time past.

Raccoon

I didn't tink broder Hum would serve me so. But, egad! I'll inform de lodge of dis! Dere's Rattletrap, too, wid his stars and t'ings— plague on dem all! And had Mrs. Placket made de fool of me too, wid her conjuring? It can't be, for I t'ink she lobes me, or she wouldn't call me her Coony and her cock-a-dandy. Dad, I'll get a bottle of her water and carry it to Dr. Witt's—den I'll know if she's a conjuror or not.[75]

Trushoop

Augh! I t'ought I should be canonicled for a shaint, but it's all over. Arra! Curse these generations of snakes—I mane wipers.

Washball

Oh, I am abused! I shall die! Oh dear, I shall die!
(*Lifting up his hands.*)

Poor Washball, disappointed Washball.
(*Hum, Quadrant, Parchment and Rattletrap alternately calling "canoe," Washball chasing them about the stage and endeavoring to strike them with the cane.*)
Get out of my house! you villains!
(*They call, "canoe."*)
You cursed villains!
("*Canoe*" *again.*)
You dogs!
("*Canoe.*")
You hell hounds!
("*Canoe.*")
You devils!
("*Canoe.*")
Curse you all!
("*Canoe.*")
(*They laugh and run off the stage.*)

Trushoop

Arra, this is the devil's own works, and they're all the devil's own children, by my showl! And they'll do great pannance for this.
(*Sings.*)
Air XVI. "The Milking Pail."
(*To be sung slow, and with an Irish accent.*)

I

Arra, what a fool was I! By my showl, I think I'll cry,
When I spake of all thish, it encrases my blish;
    'Twill kill me afore I die.
Fait', I'll not show my faash, t'escape all disgraash,
    For me they'll make a true jast.
        No more will my foes,
        Drive me by my nose,
        In bogs o'er my toes,
        And carry the ampty chast.
Augh! Feel my back is quite sore, fait', becaze it
    made me roar,
How it broke all my bones, by pulling bricks and stone,

To the mill from Washball's door.
To bear the pain and smart, I gale just in my heart
My fut is both sick and lame.
With canew and boat,
I've muddied my coat,
My wife'll cut my thro't,
The de'el take the tote;
Augh me! They'll make a great game.

McSnip

De'el dom 'em aw'.

Raccoon

Dis, dis is my own fau't for being too credulous. I put too much confidence in dose I t'ought my friends, and they deceibed me. Had I been satisfied wid my station and followed a birtuous course of life, den I might have been happy to dis day, and had not'ing to trouble my peace ob mind. But now I hab seen my folly and former bickedness, I bill take de resolution to lead a new life and follow my bus'ness wid honesty and industry, and hab not'ing more to say to de banities, bexations and alewments of dis world, which pa't I will pursue to de end of my day.

McSnip

Confusion to the vullains! I must e'en gang and put up my shapboord agen.

Washball

Oh, dear, I am robbed of my money, my health and my ease— nothing's left for me now but to grieve and lament. How shall I procure my peace again? Let me see . . . attend my business . . . what then? If a customer should laugh under the operation of my razor—egad! I should think he aimed at me for being this silly old fool, and ten to one but I might cut his throat for madness! Dress a wig? Ha! I should think my blocks grin at me—I'll instantly go and burn them all! If I hear the noise of children in the street I shall think they bawl "canoe, canoe"—confound this word! I'd give five hundred pounds it was made high treason to utter it— then I would hang every one of those cursed rogues! Oh dear, what can I do? If I rail against them publicly I shall only have the cold comfort of, " 'Tis a piece of diversion, nothing else." Hellish diversion! Suppose I should try to laugh it off—alas! alas, I can't do it!

I shan't be in a laughing humor these seven years, I'm afraid.
(*Enter Meanwell and Lucy.*)
(*They kneel.*)

Meanwell

Sir, we crave your blessing.

Washball

Go to the devil, you dog!

Trushoop

Augh! Lucy, sure you're not married?

Lucy

It is so, Mr. Trushoop. Pray endeavor to pacify my uncle.
(*Speaking to them all.*)
Pray, gentlemen, interpose.

Washball

Oh, the gipsy! I shall run stark, staring mad.

Raccoon

Come, come Mr. Washball, how can you be so angry wid her?
She's a pretty young cretur.

Meanwell

Pray, sir, pardon us.

Lucy

Pray, uncle, give us your blessing.

Trushoop

Let me entrate you, sir, to blass 'em.

Washball

I charge you both—tell me the truth! Are you really married?

Meanwell

'Tis really so, sir.

Lucy

Dear uncle, it's true.

Washball

Oh dear! Oh, lackaday! Well, if the knot is tied there's no untying
it now.

McSnip

> Come, come, man, gi'e 'em your blessing. Troth, she's a smirky, bonny lass.

Washball

> Well, since it is so, God bless you both. Rise—but remember, children, that bare walls make giddy housewives.

Meanwell

> Sir, we thank you for your kind condescension, and I must now inform you that I have this day received a letter from Jamaica giving an account of my uncle's death, enclosing a copy of his will by which, I understand, he hath left me five thousand pounds in cash, with all his real and personal property—a part of which cash is remitted me in the brig *Welcome*, Captain Trusty.[76]

Washball

> I am glad to hear it—it revives my drooping spirits.

Meanwell

> Notwithstanding this flush of fortune, I bear the same respect to your niece as heretofore, and you may depend, sir, I shall always make it my study to merit your esteem.

Washball

> You have my blessing, and may you live comfortably together, and see many happy days, and be blessed with a train of dutiful children to comfort you in your old age. And—oh!—that I, who have but one foot in the grave and the other scarcely out, had been contented, then I should have been happy in my old age and not have involved myself in this labyrinth of trouble and confusion! But let it be a warning to others not to listen to idle schemes and give way to vain imaginations, which have nearly proved fatal to me. For he whose desires are unbounded, and is weak enough to listen to artful, designing men, stands upon a dangerous precipice whose foundation must sink and he inevitably perish.
> (*Sings.*)
> *Air XVII.* "Ah! Who is me, poor Walley cried."
> (*To be sung slow.*)
>> Ah! Who is me, poor wretched I,
>>> With broken heart and downcast eyes;
>> To ease my mind where shall I fly?

A prey to knaves, poor Washball dies.
Let future generations take,
　　Example by my dismal fall,
No gods of gold, or idols make,
　　So shun the fate of poor Washball.

And now, my friends, Mr. Trushoop, Mr. McSnip and Mr. Raccoon, I expect you will honor us with your company at dinner. We'll strive to make ourselves as merry as we can, and forget our folly. Gabriel, call in the neighbors, bring your fiddle and play for us, and we'll have a dance.

Gabriel

(*Without.*)
I will, sir, sorrow on me but I will, for we haven't had a dance since last Christmas.

Washball

In the meanwhile, children, give us a song.
Air XVIII. "The Jolly Bacchanalian."
　　Banish sorrow, welcome joy,
　　　　Let's strike up the sprightly dance;
　　Mirth abound without allay;
　　　　Tune your lutes, your pipes advance;
　　Sound your notes in lofty strains,
　　Join, ye nymphs and jovial swains,
　　Banish care and be at rest,
　　Of a bad bargain make the best. Banish care, *etc.*
(*Lucy sings.*)
　　Room for joy, how blessed am I,
　　　　In a husband and a friend,
　　Virtuous joy shall never die,
　　　　Though our lives will surely end.
　　Virgins all, example take;
　　Virtue love, for virtue's sake,
　　Constant be as turtle dove,
　　Let your theme be virtuous love. Constant be, *etc.*
(*Enter Gabriel with his fiddle, and Neighbors: they strike up a country dance called "Excuse Me." After the dance Washball says:*)

Washball

> In search of treasure we are led astray,
> Believing fully what deceivers say.
> They tread unsure, who 'gainst their senses run,
> False steps pursue and rush to be undone,
> Cursed by themselves, laughed at by everyone.

(*Exeunt.*)

EPILOGUE[77]

(*Enter Hum, singing.*)

Hum

Down derry, derry down, down, down, derry.
(*Enter Rattletrap.*)

Rattletrap

Master Hum, methinks you're wonderous merry.

Hum

Gad, so I am.

Rattletrap

That I can plainly see.
(*Enter Quadrant.*)

Quadrant

Of all the plays I ever saw or heard—

Rattletrap

This beats them all, I swear now by my beard.
(*Stroking his beard.*)
(*Enter Placket.*)

Placket

'Tis false, you conjuring rogue—'tis sorry stuff.

Hum

Your servant, ma'am, for you make noise enough.
(*Hum, Quadrant and Rattletrap leave her, bowing.*)
(*Enter Topinlift.*)

Topinlift

Zounds! What's this? The devil and all to pay!
Broadside and broadside, damned warm work today!
I'll drop astern and let them end the fray.
(*He goes out backwards.*)

Placket

'Tis nonsense all, methinks I heard some say,
But hang 'em! How they laughed and clapped away.

There's one hoarse voice he croaked, " 'Tis very witty,"
A female next squeaked out, " 'Tis vastly pretty."
"Lord!" says a third, "how it alarms the city."
Plague on them all! Oh, how I shall be teased!
(*Enter Meanwell and Lucy, locked arm in arm, and cross the stage.*)

Lucy

Encircled in thy arms oh, how I'm pleased!
(*Enter Washball.*)

Washball

Confound the play! It's made a wonderous racket.

Placket

Oh, split them all, through breeches, coat and jacket!
(*She cries.*)
(*Enter Raccoon.*)

Raccoon

Come, don't cry, pet, don't cry, my pretty Placket.

Washball

Oh, monstrous! Laugh! And not one word of sense.
(*Enter McSnip.*)

McSnip

But you see, men, it pleased the audience.

Placket

Aye, to be sure—but 'twas at our expense.
(*Cries.*)

Washball

What fools they've made of us! Oh, dear! Oh, dear!
(*Enter Trushoop.*)

Trushoop

That's true for you! But, by my showl, 'twas queer.

Washball

Oh, shame! Oh, shame! My rage is to excess!

Quadrant
> (*Without.*)
> The boxes laughed aloud—you heard, I guess?

Washball
> 'Twill drive me crazy—it's a mortal blow.

Rattletrap
> (*Without.*)
> Ne'er fear, old cock—a'digging we'll all go.

Washball
> Ridiculous scenes they were transacting.

Hum
> (*Without.*)
> Pray, who made you a judge? What said the pit?

Rattletrap
> They laughed aloud, and took a deal of notice.

Hum
> One girl—I thought—ha, ha!—she's split her bodice!

Parchment
> (*Without.*)
> The boxes clapped—the ladies cried, "Bless me!"

Quadrant
> (*Without.*)
> So pleased they were, they laughed out, "Hee, hee, hee."

Washball
> That dog Hum's a very wicked body.

Hum
> (*Sings.*)
> Tol de rol, lol de rol, tol de rol loddy.

Washball
> Come, come away, for this will never do.
> Good night to ye all.

Hum
> Canoe.

Parchment
    Canoe.

Rattletrap
    Canoe.

FINIS

Notes to the Play

Title Page

1. *"Enchanting gold! . . ."* I have been unable to find the source of this quatrain, and must therefore conclude that it is original to the play. It was a convention of the eighteenth century to include an appropriate quotation, preferably by a classic author, as a motto for the play. The purpose of this quotation was to state the theme of the work if possible, or to set the tone of the play in general. It also often had the secondary function of improving the literary atmosphere that surrounded a published work, by allying the drama with the thought of the classic world.

Preface

2. "The Author's Preface to the Public." This is another standard requirement of the eighteenth-century literary scene: the lengthy disclaimer of egotistic motives for the work to follow. Many writers of the period found it necessary to deprecate the worth of their work, or to claim with admirable modesty that it was being published as a result of irresistible public desire. Too, it was the function of a dramatic preface to offer a rationale for the work's existence; in this case Forrest attributes his piece to his deeply felt interest in curtailing public folly.

3. *". . . they should be deprived of what is most valuable in a muskrat. . . ."* This is, of course, a reference to its hide or skin, a staple of the fur industry in this country since the seventeenth century. Trapping muskrats along Delaware Bay was a large industry in the eighteenth century, particularly during the winter months when the pelts were thickest. Forrest's reference to the burrowing habits of muskrats is founded upon fact: "where the banks of streams have some elevation they (muskrats) form extensive burrows. . . . The excavations are of great injury to artificial embankments along canals and rivers, by permitting the water to undermine . . . them, and in some parts of the country they do serious damage to canal embankments and riverbanks" (*Encyclopedia Americana*).

Prologue

4. It was quite often the case in the eighteenth century to have the prologue of a new work written by a distinguished writer, or someone of high position in the dramatic community. The function of a prologue was manifold: it could serve as an opportunity for the author to address the public directly on social practices or manners, it could be used as a vehicle for dramatic theories and opinions, or it could be a bid for a good hearing from the audience. In each event, a subsidiary purpose of the prologue was literary justification for the play's existence

114

and, like the preface in the published editions, it served to elevate the art of playwriting.

We don't know if Forrest wrote the prologue to *The Disappointment*; it seems likely that he did, as there are no other claimants. As a prologue, it is typical in that it restates the purpose of the theater as a social and ethical corrective and asks for a good hearing. It is interesting to see that Forrest seems to be aware of the fact that his play would be the first to be professionally produced in America, but aside from that the prologue lacks value.

The somewhat smarmy bid for approval in the last couplet has a long history in the theater; asking for applause is a device at least as old as Plautus. Not even Shakespeare was free from this convention, although typically he asks for it in the epilogue of *The Tempest* with wry humor and without condescension.

The prologue was often spoken by the comic lead, if it was in fact employed in the actual production and not written solely for the published edition. By whom it was to be spoken in this instance is not indicated, nor is the speaker characterized by the language as was the case with Goldsmith, for example, later on.

5. *"Nor gall or copp'ras tincture her design."* Gall, "an excrescence produced on trees, esp. the oak . . . largely used in the manufacture of ink and tannin, as well as in dyeing and in medicine" (*Shorter Oxford English Dictionary*) was the botanical equivalent of copperas, "a name given from ancient times to the sulphates of copper, iron, or zinc . . . used in dyeing, tanning, or making ink" (*Shorter Oxford English Dictionary*). Both of these elements are noted for their corrosive bitterness, a quality that Forrest suggests (with truth) will be lacking in the satire he is going to present.

Dramatis Personae

6. *Characters' names.* The majority of the characters have "title-names," by which something of their character, occupation, or social position is exposed to the audience. "Quadrant," for example, refers to the navigational instrument used, like the modern sextant, to measure the height of a celestial object from the horizon. To this characterization of Quadrant, Forrest adds no other appropriate verbal symbols of the instrument-maker's trade or any internal reference to the label-name other than Quadrant's becoming responsible for the instruments used in the hoax. Quadrant the character is modeled upon "an old instrument-maker, by name Cappock."

The label-name "Raccoon" has been discussed in the introduction, while "Washball" is a reference to that character's occupation, hairdressing and barbering. A washball was a sponge, covered with a soft cloth, used in the bath, and barbershops used to have public bathrooms.

"Trushoop" also gives us the occupation of the character—a cooper, or barrel-maker. A truss hoop is the large metal band first put around the staves of a barrel to force and keep them in position.

The sailor "Topinlift" has the name of a piece of sailing tackle. More properly "topping lift," the term describes a line that is used to support one of the smaller spars on a sailing ship, and to relieve the halyard of some of the weight of the spar and its sail when they are raised or lowered.

A "placket" is, archaically, a "slit in a woman's garment" (*Webster's Third International Dictionary*) and, by extension, a reference to the vagina.

It was the custom, in plays of this period, to separate the male from the female characters and to list them somewhat arbitrarily. In this instance, for example, the male characters are listed in order of appearance (with the exception of Terence and Gabriel, who are included in the list of supernumeraries as "servants"), while the women are listed in no particular order. I confess not to know the origin or reasoning for this segregation or arrangement.

Act I, scene i

7. "*Scene opens and discovers. . . .*" It may be remembered that the main curtain of an eighteenth-century theater was raised before the action of the play began and remained so until the end, unlike the modern practice of lowering it for act and scene breaks. In this instance the curtain would have risen on an empty stage, with the midstage shutters in place, perhaps depicting the rustic exterior to be used later. The prologue was delivered before this setting, the character who recited it having entered through one of the proscenium doors downstage. After the prologue the actor would exit—let us hope to some applause—and the midstage shutters would be drawn back, revealing, or "discovering," the humorists seated around a table.

As there were no programs with a synopsis of the scenes, the eighteenth-century playwright was required to establish a place through the action or dialogue. Forrest performs this expository chore quite well—with the wine pouring, the drinking song, the large tavern table—and does not waste dialogue telling the audience where the scene is supposed to be. It is a small point, but nonetheless an indication of Forrest's technical skill.

8. "*So far we have sailed before the wind. . . .*" A nautical metaphor for "having an easy time of it." When one sails before the wind in a square-rigged ship, the wind is directly at one's back, pushing the ship. Square-rigged ships, as opposed to the fore-and-aft-rigged modern sailboats, operated most efficiently when being pushed by the wind directly behind them. Sailing before the wind is quite smooth as well, with little of the pitching and yawing that accompany other points of sailing—so the metaphor is well chosen.

9. "*Trushoop speaks of building a chapel. . . .*" This must have struck predominantly Protestant Philadelphia as an eccentric plan, to say the least. The city had two Roman Catholic churches at the time of *The Disappointment*—St. Joseph's, a tiny chapel on the edge of Shippen's apple orchard, and the much more elaborate St. Mary's, built in 1763—and the contemplated addition of a third would probably have been greeted with derision. After all, there were fewer than 200 Catholics in Philadelphia at the time, and anti-Catholic prejudice was a fact of life in the city. The more tolerant audience members would possibly have reacted to Trushoop's plan with wry amusement at the incomprehensible actions of a Papist, while others may well have seen in it something sinister and worthy of contempt. (See Kelley, *Life and Times in Colonial Philadelphia*, pp. 146–47.)

10. ". . . *the canto of Hudibras and Sydrophel. . . .*" A reference to the tremendously popular mock-heroic poem *Hudibras*, by Samuel Butler. Begun in 1663 and completed in 1678 with the publication of *Hudibras, Part III*, Butler's

poem is a broad satiric attack on Puritanism, chronicling the adventures of Hudibras's encounter with "a Rosicrucian prognosticator," Sydrophel, and mocks the absurd affectations of astrology and divination.

Butler's writing has been described as "burlesque, through distortion, and travesty, through vulgarization." It is not difficult to understand why his style and method would have appealed to Forrest as well as to the humorists. (See Baugh et al., *A Literary History of England*, p. 375.)

11. "*. . . a hazel-rod off our cherry tree, a magnet, nocturnal, and forestaff . . .*" The "hazel-rod" was a wand, or more likely a divining rod for finding water or buried objects. "Magnet" is used in the sense of "compass." A "nocturnal" was "an astronomical instrument for taking observations by which to ascertain the hour of the night" (*Oxford English Dictionary*), and a "forestaff," or more properly a cross-staff, was a crude navigational instrument for measuring the altitude of the sun or a star (*Oxford English Dictionary*). Nocturnals and forestaffs looked complex and would have impressed those who did not know their function as being mysterious and suspicious machines.

12. "*Moon dial, and Napier's bones. . . .*" The moon dial was used, like the nocturnal, to tell time at night. Napier's bones were "narrow slips of bone, ivory, wood, *etc.*, divided into compartments marked with certain digits, and used to facilitate the variations of multiplication and division according to a method invented by John Napier, 1550–1617" (*Oxford English Dictionary*)—in other words, a primitive adding machine. All of these instruments would make impressive "props" to fool the dupes.

13. "*Broder Hum. . . .*" The use of the title identifies Raccoon and Hum as Masons.

14. (*Aside.*) This stage direction is a convention that the theater no longer employs. The actor, speaking "aside," would say something either to himself or to the audience that presumably, the other characters onstage could not hear. Parenthetically, in giving the aside the actor did not change the voice nor did he speak from behind his hand, as stage villains are invariably depicted as doing in the popular imagination.

15. (*He knocks.*) This was the usual method of calling a servant in a public place, by rapping with one's heel or cane on the floor. The next stage direction, in which the Drawer speaks from "below," is ambiguous. It could refer to the physical placement of the actor playing the servant, i.e., literally below the stage; but it also could have been intended by Forrest in a nontheatrical sense, to indicate that the humorists and dupes are in a private room on the second floor of the tavern. It is my feeling that the two stage directions refer to the place of the action rather than the physical position of the actor playing the servant. While the Southwark Theater probably had a space under the stage for the necessary trapdoor openings, and for use as dressing rooms, it would be unnecessary for the Drawer to actually go there to speak his lines before he enters. It is highly likely that Forrest was succumbing to literalness, in indicating the realistic actions and responses in taverns of the time.

16. "*. . . or by St. Andra'. . . .*" More properly, Saint Andrew, the patron saint of Scotland.

17. "*Gentlemen! I expected when I was sent for. . . .*" This long and quite funny speech has already been discussed in the introduction. Like the sign over Rip's favorite tavern in "Rip Van Winkle," Parchment's political loyalties change

with great smoothness. It may be of interest to compare his legalistic tirade with the version in the second edition of *The Disappointment*, revised and published in 1796:

Parchment

    (*Starting up suddenly.*)

    Gentlemen! I expected when I was invited here it was to take a cheerful glass with my friends. I had no idea of a secret to be divulged—not I—and I earnestly request that if it is any scheme, plot, association, combination, machination, contrivance, secret conclave, cabal, privy conspiracy, rout, riot, rebellious meeting or unlawful assembly—in fine, if it is anything against the illustrious President of the United States, or of the Society of Cincinnati—whom God preserve!—the honorable the Vice President of the honorable Senate—the honorable the Senate collectively, or individually—the honorable the House of Representatives of the United States, that standing bulwark of American freedom, in Congress assembled or not assembled, or either of them—The honorable the Secretary of State—The honorable the Secretary of the Treasury—The honorable the Secretary of War—The honorable the Chief Justice of the United States—The honorable the associate judges in their judicial capacities or otherwise—The honorable the Attorney General of the United States—the Right Reverend the bishops and clergy of the United States of all denominations, whether in church or out of it—the constitution, laws, and government under which we live—To be brief, I say, gentlemen, if it is any scheme, plot, association, combination, machination, contrivance, secret conclave, cabal, privy conspiracy, rout, riot, rebellious meeting or unlawful assembly aforesaid once more—keep it to yourselves, don't let me know a tittle of it! I wash my hands of it—for if I know it, I'll be a swift witness against you! As I profess myself a worthy citizen, a true republican, a man of honor and a gentleman by birth and education, I'll immediately to the Attorney-General, lodge a complaint against you and hang you every mother's son!

A comparison of these two statements, separated by twenty-nine years, is a sociopolitical study *in petto*.

    18. "... *his most sacred majesty, George the Second*. ..." A curious reference, as George II died in 1760, seven years before the writing of *The Disappointment*. Several explanations for this anachronism have been suggested. It could have been a misprint, or an indication that the news of George's death had not yet reached the colonies; neither of these is tenable. Another possibility is that Forrest deliberately used the late king as a referent in order to place the action of the play in the past, thus partially removing some of the contemporaneity of the satire. This explanation strikes me as overly subtle; the Philadelphia audience, had there been one, would probably have taken the reference as a mistake on either the actor's or the playwright's part.

    It has also been suggested that the practical joke that was the basis of *The Disappointment* took place at least seven years before the writing of the play. This seems as unreasonable as the other explanations, if only because Forrest would have been only thirteen years old at the time, somewhat young to play an elaborate joke of this nature on his elders.

I am convinced that the reference is deliberate and that the reasons for setting the play in the past are complex. Contemporaneity was not as desirable in the eighteenth-century theater as it seems to be today. Forrest may have understood this, if only partially, and felt that the quality of the play would be improved if he could establish the action as having taken place in the recent past. Paul Hostetler has suggested an interesting explanation for Forrest's employment of the late king, based on the then-current unpopularity of George III and his councillors. "The author may not have wished," Professor Hostetler has proposed, "to put an unpopular declaration of allegiance in the mouth of one of the principal and sympathetic agents of his play, even though the protest is a hypocritical one." There is much to be said for this suggestion.

19. ". . . *as great a regord*. . . ." There is an intriguing ambiguity about this line, particularly when one considers that many of the Scots in North America at this time loathed the House of Hanover and its works as a result of the destruction of the Jacobite cause by the English in 1745. Churchill tells us in his *History of the English-Speaking People* that "Scottish-Irish refugees . . . formed a strong English-hating element in their new homes" (3:121). On the other hand, loyalty to the crown was still strong in colonial America among some of the Scotch-Irish immigrants, particularly as a result of the power of the Scottish lords in the government of George II, under the leadership of Lord Bute.

Consequently, the line can be taken as ironic or sincere; it certainly would have provoked some response from the audience, in large measure because of their feelings toward McSnip as a representative of a minority. The same can be said for Parchment's response to McSnip's protest of loyalty; as written, it is charged with ambiguity and would depend upon an actor's interpretation to be made unequivocal.

20. "*Arra, my dear*. . . ." The word *arra* has no definitive meaning and is used by the Irish (particularly on the stage) as an indeterminate sound to express enthusiasm for the statement that follows. An American equivalent would be the sentence prefix "Boy" used indiscriminately by adolescents in the recent past.

This line also contains the first of many "Irish bulls" delivered by Trushoop. An Irish bull is a statement that is self-contradictory or impossible. Trushoop's lines are littered with these curiosities to the point of becoming somewhat tedious.

21. ". . . *the famous Captain Blackbeard*. . . ." The pirate Edward Teach, better known then and now as Blackbeard, held a fascination for Americans of that time. Exploits bordering on the marvelous were attributed to him by many writers and commentators of the period, and he quickly became a legend closely comparable to Billy the Kid or Jesse James, although more malevolent than they. In reality, Teach was a criminally insane murderer, thief, and racketeer who flourished on the North Carolina and Virginia coasts from late 1716 until his death on November 21, 1718. During his brief career Blackbeard achieved a reputation for evil and depravity second to none. He did much to foster fear and loathing among the colonists upon whom he preyed by his bizarre appearance and actions. Charles Roberts, in *A Generall History of the Robberies and Murders of the most notorious Pyrates* (1724) describes him thus: ". . . in time of Action, he wore a Sling over his Shoulders, with three brace of Pistols, hanging in Holsters like Bandoliers; he wore a Fur-Cap, and stuck a lighted Match on each side under it, which appearing on each side his Face, his Eyes naturally

looking Fierce and Wild, made him altogether such a Figure, that Imagination cannot form an Idea of a Fury, from Hell, to look more frightful."

Teach acquired the name Blackbeard not only from the color of his abundant facial hair but from his manner of wearing it: "He was wont to plait the beard into little tails, the ends of which he tied with fanciful colored ribbons. Some of these braids he twisted back over his ears" (Hugh S. Rankin, *The Golden Age of Piracy* [Williamsburg, Va., 1969], p. 108.) The effect of this grotesque and horrifying figure on the imagination of Americans was tremendous. Rankin quotes a contemporary of Blackbeard who said that the pirate "frightened America more than any Comet that has appeared there for a long time" (p. 108).

It is important to note that the mere mention of buried treasure, particularly treasure buried by Blackbeard, is sufficient to convince the dupes in *The Disappointment* that the trove is buried nearby. The Delaware River and its bay were the scene of sporadic pirate activity in the late seventeenth and early eighteenth centuries and, as Forrest noted in the introduction to *The Disappointment*, hunting for buried treasure became a highly popular activity toward the middle of the eighteenth. Franklin found the activities of the treasure hunters sufficiently foolish to comment upon them as early as 1729. Blackbeard himself was reported to have visited Philadelphia in 1713—although this is highly unlikely—and was said to have kept a house on Marcus Hook in which he stored his ill-gotten gains and "kept many a revel." On this point William M. Mervine's "Pirates and Privateers in the Delaware Bay and River" (PMHB 32 [1908]:459–70) has been most helpful and should be consulted by the interested reader. Furthermore, piratical acts were troublesome in the Philadelphia region as late as 1747—sufficiently troublesome that the Pennsylvania Assembly was asked to equip ships to defend the Delaware Bay from the pirates. (The Assembly refused.) See Charles J. Stillé, "The Attitude of the Quakers in the Provincial Wars," PMHB 10 (1886):291.

Thus, we see that the dupes' credulity in accepting the "Blackbeard papers" unquestioningly is well within the realm of possibility, and indeed only reflects the tremendous interest taken in the activities of Blackbeard—both real and invented—at that time. The dupes are not fools, they are merely typical.

22. *"Imprimis, seventeen golden candlesticks. . . ."* This description is completely fantastic. There are no records to suggest that Blackbeard had ever accumulated goods of this amount in his entire career. Perhaps the greatest amount ever captured by pirates came from Henry Morgan's sacking of Panama, where the loot was estimated to require 175 mules to transport it.

It is quite impossible to estimate the modern worth of this highly imaginative treasure-trove, but a few modern equivalents may be of interest: a pistole was a Spanish coin worth about twenty-five shillings at the time, and approximately three dollars today; a pistareen was one-half a pistole. The treasure, then, consisted of almost half a million dollars in those coins alone, and it should be remembered that the buying power of the money at the time was anywhere from two-and-a-half to three times what it is today. In view of these figures, Washball's response seems a little subdued.

23. *". . . signed by Edward Teach, alias Blackbeard, captain. . . ."* The horrific names of the crew have some basis in historical practice. Pirates and privateers of the period quite often assigned themselves bloodcurdling names. John Hyde Preston, in his *Short History of the American Revoluton* (New York,

1953), gives us the officers' list for the British privateer *Terrible*—"Captain Death, Lieutenants Spirit and Ghost, Boatswain Butcher, Quartermaster Debbil"— and states that the ship was "launched out of Execution Dock, London" (p. 295).

24. ". . . *oh hon'acree. . . .*" Another Gaelic expression of affection, with no more precise meaning than the present-day "baby," when applied to adults.

25. ". . . *and keck the shap-boord oot 'a' the wandow.*" A shop-board was a low table upon which tailors sat while at work. It was a symbol of the tailor's trade, and McSnip is suggesting in his violent way that he will leave his trade. This decision could not have sat well with many in the audience; Philadelphians of that time believed strongly, for the most part, in Poor Richard's adage "Keep thy shop and thy shop will keep thee."

26. "*Father Duffy never made a better.*" There was no Roman Catholic priest named Duffy in Philadelphia at the time of *The Disappointment*. An English Jesuit, Father Harding, was the pastor of the only Catholic church, St. Mary's. Perhaps Forrest invented the Irish priest for consistency's sake.

27. ". . . *two pistoles a man.*" Approximately five dollars a man—not a "trifling" sum, as Rattletrap calls it, particularly in terms of the buying power of money in 1767, but by no means exorbitant. It is a good price for Forrest to charge, as it were, for it emphasizes the fact that the humorists are not trying to extort but merely to humiliate.

28. "*Mashah, my dear!*" Another Gaelic sentence prefix; see note 20.

Act I, scene ii

29. "*By the Holy Stone. . . .*" A holy stone was any rock or stone cross that had particular religious significance in Ireland. Innumerable stones in that country have been blessed by the presence of a saint in the myriad local traditions. Trushoop is not referring to one holy object in particular, but is making a generalized, mild oath.

30. ". . . *holy Saint Dominick, Saint Patrick, Saint Kullumkill. . . .*" There are many Saint Dominicks, but Trushoop is probably referring to Dominic Guzmán (?–1221), founder of the Dominicans. Saint Patrick is the patron saint of Ireland, and Saint Kullumkill is more properly Saint Columcille or Columba, the second most important religious figure in Celtic history. Born in 521, he was a missionary to Scotland as well as the founder of many churches there and in Ireland. He died in 597.

31. ". . . *the cooper's march. . . .*" The regular sound that a barrel-maker makes, driving nails through the hoops of a barrel into the staves.

32. ". . . *the Earl of Portleydown's own wife.*" There is no earl of Portleydown in the British or Irish peerage, nor has there been in the past. There is no Portleydown as a place name in Ireland, but there is a Portglenone, which Forrest may have heard of and misunderstood. It is a small town in County Antrim, on the River Bann. However there is no title connected with it.

It has been impossible to identify Lady Barrymoore. There was an earl of Barrymore, David Fitz-David Barry (1605–42), whose title was not inherited by either of his sons after his death during the Civil War (*Dictionary of National Biography*, 1:1233). I suspect that Forrest simply used the names for their Irish quality, rather than for any real contemporary associations they may have had.

33. ". . . *the pashence of Saint Ignatius or the Holy Pope.* . . ." Saint Ignatius is Ignatius Loyola, founder of the Society of Jesus in 1534. Clement XIII
was pope at the time of *The Disappointment.* Neither of these men had any
particular reputation for extraordinary patience; indeed, Loyola was known to be
quite short-tempered.

34. *"Dad, I'll put.* . . ." "Dad" is a corruption of "Egad," which is in turn a
distortion of "The God," a mild oath.

35. ". . . *when she come to see broder Solomon.*" Raccoon's familiarity with
Solomon stems from a belief held by many Masons that their order originated
with stonemasons involved in the building of the Great Temple of Jerusalem in
the tenth century B.C. Thus, by extension, Solomon could be considered the
founder of Freemasonry.

36. (*Within.*) In theatrical parlance, this means backstage. Probably Raccoon
would enter from one side of the stage, directly above one of the sets of wings,
to indicate that he had come from outside. Placket would enter from the opposite
side of the stage, to indicate that she was coming from another part of the house.

37. *"Air IV.* 'Yankee Doodle.'" This is the earliest reference we have to this
historically important song, and its inclusion in the play indicates that it was
popular long before the Revolution, when, as tradition has had it, it became
popular as a jeering reference to the rebels. See David Ewen's *American Popular
Songs* (New York, 1966) for a brief description of the history of "Yankee
Doodle." Ewen's book is accurate in many respects, although small mistakes (e.g.,
his reference to the song being "interpolated in an early American comic opera,
The Disappointment of Andrew Barton" [p. 452]) are disquieting.

38. ". . . *we're all to meet at the Ton* [sic]. . . ." A reference to the Tun
Tavern on Water Street, one of Philadelphia's most popular taverns. The Tun was
noted for its food, and finds a footnote in history as the birthplace both of
American Masonry in 1732 and the United States Marines in 1775.

Act I, scene iii

39. (*He makes a cut at the brass knob.* . . .) There is very little reason to believe that this action on McSnip's part would actually have taken place on the
stage, had the play been produced. Scenery in the eighteenth-century theater had
not progressed to the point of three-dimensional decoration, as the mentioning of
a real brass doorknob would imply. Without doubt this is an example of Forrest's
lack of professional experience in the theater. Though a funny bit of business, it
is doubtful that Douglass would have had the desire or the facilities to stage it.

The rest of the dialogue reflects Forrest's occasionally good ear for dialect.
McSnip is quite excited, and the brogue dialogue becomes thicker and more
abrupt as his fury mounts. The items he wishes to do "awa' " with, "ste'tepe,
bookrum, mooneer, guze, shares and aw' " are articles and tools of his trade,
now despised. *Stay-tape* was a narrow strip of cloth used to cover the hard stays
in the waists of dresses; *buckram* is a gauze impregnated with starch or sizing
and used to stiffen or strengthen collars, lapels, and the like; while a *mooneer* was
a crescent-shaped knife used to scrape, thin, and soften leather. "Shares" is Mc-
Snip's pronunciation of *shears.*

40. "... *nawthing less than Loord Chaumberlin.* . . ." This is possibly an oblique reference to John Stuart, third earl of Bute, a malign influence on the young George III. Bute, a Scotsman, had been groom of the stole to George's mother, Augusta of Saxe-Gotha, and with the death of George II became extremely influential in the court, although he lacked an official capacity until 1761 when he was appointed secretary of state. Later in the century Bute was to become one of the prime villains in the Revolutionary demonology (see Philbrick, pp. 42–44). This semipolitical reference is one of the similarities that Sonneck finds between *The Disappointment* and *The Fall of British Tyranny* (see his introduction, p. 65). In the latter play Bute is characterized as a Machiavellian villain of tremendous proportions. I remain convinced, however, that Forrest's implication with McSnip's ambitions is not political, but rather proceeds from a desire to gain a laugh from common gossip—in this case from the comparison of McSnip to another Scotsman who "made good."

41. "... *a Knight of the Golden Fleece.*" "After the Order of the Garter, the most famous order of knighthood in Europe" (Grant Uden, *A Dictionary of Chivalry* [New York, 1968], p. 106). The order was founded in 1430 by Philip the Good, Duke of Burgundy, to commemorate his marriage to Isabella of Portugal. In the eighteenth century both the Austrian and Spanish sovereigns awarded the Toison d'Or as their "principal order of knighthood . . . exclusively reserved to Catholics of the highest nobility" (*Encyclopedia Brittanica*, 13:406). It would seem that Washball would have little chance of achieving his goal, even if the treasure were real.

42. "... *settle a good jointure on her.*" "The holding of property to the joint use of husband and wife for life or in tail, as a provision for the latter during widowhood. Hence, a sole estate limited to the wife, to take effect upon the death of her husband for her whole life at least" (*Oxford English Dictionary*).

Act I, scene vii

43. "*I had engaged with Mr. Trappick.* . . ." There was no one of this name engaged in financial activities in Philadelphia at that time. Doubtless Forrest is using a label-name here again, in this case "Traffick," made more confusing by Raccoon's accent. The term *traffick* meant exchange, or business intercourse. To estimate the value of the treasure, use these figures and the information in note 22.

44. "... *dollughons.*" This word does not appear in a Gaelic dictionary. It has been suggested to me that it is a stage-Irish pronunciation of "hooligans," and while I am not at all satisfied with this suggestion, I have been unable to offer a better.

45. "... *on board a canoe.*" It should be remembered that the term *canoe* at the time referred not only to the small, double-ended boat used by the Indians, but also to any boat whose hull was made from a hollowed log, if only in part. On some occasions these dugout canoes were of considerable size; Penn himself wrote: "I have a canoe of one tree it fetches four tunns of bricks." The treasure chest could easily have been conveyed in a canoe of the size Penn suggests. It is also of interest to note the indigenous quality of the word chosen by the "humorists"; it helps to intensify the American flavor of the work. Too, there is a comic

element in the sound of the word *canoe*; the final syllable can be elongated to humorous effect. It was a good choice for a password.

46. ". . . *p'whillalew at the sight of the talf*. . . ." "P'whillalew" is an attempt to write "fa, la, la" as it might be pronounced by an Irishman, while *talf* is a mistaken substitution for *pelf*, i.e., money.

47. ". . . *fiddle* 'Gramudgey Gramaugh'. . . ." An Irish folk song, specifically unknown to any of my sources, but probably a love song, inasmuch as *gra* is Gaelic for "love."

48. ". . . *skolrankey or good usquebaugh*." *Skolrankey* is strong ale, and *usquebaugh* is Gaelic for *aqua vitae*, or "water of life"—in these less poetic times, plain whiskey.

49. ". . . *meet at the stone bridge*." I have not been able to find a reference to a stone bridge, identified as such, in the Philadelphia area at that time. There were several bridges over various creeks that flowed to the Delaware or Schuylkill rivers, but none known specifically as "the stone bridge." If the "place of action" for the practical joke is supposed to be Petty's Island, as some have suggested, there is only one stream of any size to be passed on the way up the river to the island from Philadelphia: Quince's Run. I have been unable to determine if the bridge over this creek was of stone or wood. This problem is complicated by the fact that the great Philadelphia architect Robert Smith had proposed and designed a bridge over the Schuylkill in 1765 that was called a "stone bridge" when it was in fact wooden, the supporting piers alone being of stone. This bridge cannot be the one referred to in the play: for one thing, it did not yet exist and the audience knew it, and for another it was designed to cross a river that lay behind Philadelphia—and therefore in the opposite direction from the Delaware, where the treasure had supposedly been buried.

50. ". . . *my gauging rod*. . . ." A gauging rod was a "graduated rod for measuring with great accuracy the internal diameters of portions of work" (*Oxford English Dictionary*), and a tool therefore of great importance to a barrel-maker. There would not be the slightest use for it on a treasure hunt, but Trushoop's enthusiasm in volunteering what was perhaps his most valuable tool is somewhat touching.

51. ". . . *me andra*. . . ." McSnip is referring to his broadsword with a dialect pronunciation of "hanger," a term for any sword worn from the waist or shoulder.

Act II, scene i.

52. "*How stands the wind?*" Topinlift is asking from what direction the wind is blowing, his nautical way of asking if it is all right for him to visit Placket.

53. "*If ever I blow you, blast me!*" This entire speech is filled with sailor's slang and nautical expressions. *Head-rails* are timbers at the head (or front) of a ship, used to support the bowsprit, among other functions; the term is used here in reference to Topinlift's mouth. I have been unable to discover the meaning of *jillkicker*; it is possible that Forrest made up the word, or that he heard it incorrectly from a sailor acquaintance. There is a small possibility that it may be a corruption of "jillicker," a small sail used on coastal ships, hung from the mizzenmast. The *main-yard* is the largest spar on a square-rigged ship, from which the mainsail is hung. Sailors were required to climb up to and out on this spar

to furl the mainsail, and were sometimes blown off into the water. This practice was especially dangerous because the mainsail usually was furled only in a storm, making the work on the main-yard particularly hazardous.

54. ". . . *a damned fist in the Killecranky trade.*" The *Killecranky trade* was a slang term for smuggling. The pass of Killecranky was a favorite for smugglers in Scotland, being the easiest passage from the Highlands to Edinburgh.

55. ". . . *grappled with you.* . . ." In this instance Topinlift is using terminology from naval combat techniques: *long-shot* was, as the name implies, long-distance firing from one ship at another; it was notoriously inaccurate and inconclusive. To *grapple* with the enemy was to lay one ship alongside another and join them together with lines, so that boarding parties could be used for hand-to-hand combat; in this manner many naval engagements were settled. Topinlift, of course, does not have combat in mind.

56. (*She locks the door.*) Eighteenth-century staging was not sufficiently realistic to require real doors and locks as part of the scenery. Placket would probably have stepped quickly offstage after the line ". . . let's make the door fast first" and then reentered to continue the line. This action, coupled with the line announcing her intention, would have satisfied the audience of that time. The stage direction is therefore unnecessary, and that Forrest found it necessary is an indication of his lack of theatrical expertise.

57. ". . . *the clews of your hammock.* . . ." Clews are pieces of strong twine threaded through grommets to tie down the material to which they are attached. Usually they are placed at the edge or corner of a piece of material. On hammocks they were of course at the ends, and were used to tie the hammock to the overhead beams. What Topinlift is suggesting is that he and Placket test the strength of her bed.

58. ". . . *bowse taut my rolling tackles.*" To *bowse* is to tighten by pulling on a line, in marine terminology. *Rolling tackles* are block-and-tackle systems aboard a sailing ship that are used to trim or adjust the position of the sails. They are pulled tight in inclement weather.

59. ". . . *my uncle at Germantown.* . . ." At the time of *The Disappointment* there was a cult of mystics who called themselves "The Society of the Woman in the Wilderness," or "The Circle of Perfection." This group, founded by the German eccentric John Kelpius, lived in a cave near Germantown. Although the group dissolved after Kelpius's death in 1708, their practices and philosophy were kept alive by the unique Dr. Christopher Witt of Germantown, known locally as "the Hex-Master of Spook Hill," who professed himself able to do all the things Placket ascribes to her uncle. Although Witt was not German, I believe that Forrest probably is referring to this strange man. Later in the play Witt is named, and he obviously was a source of much humor to Forrest and his young friends. I am further convinced that Anthony Armbruster, as suggested in the introduction, may have taken exception to this reference to German almanac-makers and joined in the protest against the performance of *The Disappointment*. Watson tells us that Armbruster was interested in the magical arts to the extent that he tried to conjure a spirit as part of the original practical joke. Whether or not Armbruster was involved in the other arcane practices Placket suggests is unknown; his almanacs were locally hailed for their "telling vignettes from American history," not for any particular magical materials they might have possessed.

For many Philadelphians, Germantown had a reputation for strange goings-on, and Placket's remarks about magical doctors in that town would doubtless have produced a large, knowing laugh from the audience. For more on Dr. Witt, see Carsten E. Seecamp's "The Circle of Perfection," PMHB 94 (1970): 196–98.

60. *"Dunder schlemer hoont. . . ."* This is gibberish, as are all the foreign phrases in the play. While the words do bear some relationship to German (e.g., *dunder* for *donder* ["thunder"], and *hoont* possibly for *hund* ["dog"]), they form no coherent meaning in conjunction. Nevertheless, they sound properly emphatic and foreboding and thus accomplish the desired purpose.

61. *"Well, it's an old saying. . . ."* It is difficult to determine precisely what Placket is objecting to in this speech; superficially, she seems to be faulting Raccoon for lack of provision, yet earlier in the scene she explains to Topinlift that she abides the old debauchee for the opposite reason. Furthermore, the line "He has deceived me long enough!" hardly seems fair if the reference is to Raccoon. Any deception in their relationship is certainly all on Placket's part. The only way to make sense of this tirade is to suggest that Placket is objecting not to Raccoon's financial parsimony, but to his inability through age to provide for her physical needs, what she calls her "real necessaries." Viewed in this light, the speech becomes wickedly funny and psychologically revealing.

Act II, scene ii

62. *". . . safe in your hole."* This and other references lead us to the conclusion that the stage of the Southwark Theater must have been trapped, with openings in the stage floor to accommodate the treasure chest and Spitfire with his props. Furthermore, there must have been several traps, or at least two, for the chest is buried in one and Spitfire is placed in another. It also appears that the traps were adjustable in depth: surely the chest would not have been lowered all the way to the floor beneath the stage, for this would have been a distance of at least five feet and would have complicated the action on stage of burying and uncovering the treasure. Much of the digging must have been faked by those playing the dupes, to give the impression of depth.

These requirements were reasonably complicated for the theater of the time, and the fact that the American Company was not only willing but able to reproduce this scene physically confirms the suspicion that the Southwark was by no means the crude, jury-rigged theater its detractors would have us believe.

63. *". . . I charged my sel' wi' twa bottles. . . ."* McSnip is telling us in effect that he has prepared for the adventure by drinking two bottles to give himself courage ("to lengthen me nawse"). If the bottles contained whiskey—and it is hard to imagine a Scotsman drinking anything else—it is no wonder that he is unable to hit the "ghost" with his sword later in the scene.

64. *". . . by the Satellites. . . ."* The first of many astrological expressions used inaccurately but to great effect by Rattletrap.

65. *"The rod points to this spot."* The reference is to a divining rod, or water-witch, which is a forked stick believed by many to have the ability to find water or buried objects when held by the right person. Believers are convinced that the rod will physically pull the operator toward the buried object and will dip—sometimes violently—when it is directly above the object of the search. I cannot

comment on Rattletrap's formula for constructing his dowsing rod, but midnight on Hallowe'en seems a potent moment, and the method sufficiently mysterious to be a virtual guarantee of efficiency.

It should be noted that Forrest provides the actor with a delightful stage picture at this moment: Rattletrap, dressed in his robes and being dragged from one side of the stage to the other by the strange powers of the rod in his hands, is a spectacle that, in the hands of an experienced actor, could not fail to be hilarious.

66. "*Diapaculum interravo. . . .*" This is gibberish, for the most part, as is all of the "Latin" Rattletrap uses in this scene. While both Latin roots and endings are used, they make no sense grammatically or syntactically. Nonetheless, Forrest has made a good choice of sounds—if spoken, the nonsense gives the impression of intellectual majesty. This practice of dog-Latin spoken on the stage to impress the less learned is a timeless device of the classic stage; it dates at least to the *commedia dell'arte* of the fifteenth century.

67. ". . . *the Bachelor's Hall.*" A private clubhouse of the time. Its exact location is unknown, but it was perhaps near Marsh Street, on the north side of Philadelphia. If this is the case, then the "place of action" might have been near Petty's Island, north of the city. See Townsend Ward, "North Second Street and its Associations," PMHB 4 (1880):179–80.

68. ". . . *round the poleaster.*" What Rattletrap is saying is that the constellation of the Serpent is entangled with the North Star—an astronomic impossibility and an astrologic disaster.

69. ". . . *laid in Lake Huron. . . .*" A most interesting reference. Lake Huron had been much in the news and in the consciousness of colonial Americans during the French and Indian War and as part of the theater of operations during Pontiac's War. Lake Huron was the scene of the massacre at Fort Michilimakinac in 1763, among other claims to notoriety, and to many Philadelphians it no doubt had the reputation of being a breeding ground of monsters in the guise of Indians. Pontiac's War was concluded only three years before *The Disappointment* appeared, and in that time Pontiac and his activities around the Great Lakes had become well known in the cities of the Eastern seaboard, and were in fact becoming legend.

Rattletrap's reference to Lake Superior and Lake Huron (at the moment of raising the chest) may have been designed to identify the horrid Blackbeard with another threat to colonial America, the savage Indians of the Five Nations. It is perhaps not too much to say that the audience would have found particularly appropriate Rattletrap's choice of places in which to confine the spirit, among the Indians who had so recently threatened them.

70. ". . . *when he robbed the churches.*" Washball is confused, which is quite justified under the circumstances. Blackbeard never robbed churches in Panama or elsewhere: this is a reference to Sir Henry Morgan's sack of Panama in 1670. Washball's concern for the "poor priests" is in fact more applicable to the treatment given them by Morgan in his earlier sack of Porto Bello, on the east coast of Panama. During the pirate siege of the city in 1667, "Morgan's men used captured monks and nuns, many of whom were shot down, as living shields as they brought up scaling ladders." (Rankin, *Golden Age of Piracy*, p. 13.) It is of course impossible to determine if the confusion on Washball's part is deliberate on Forrest's. The date the playwright gives to the coin that prompts Washball's remark is accurate, and shows some chronological awareness of piratic activity.

Act II, scene iv

71. "*I'll go and inform the Collector.* . . ." The sense of this line is self-evident: Washball plans to take advantage of the regulation that allows one-half of recovered stolen goods to be rewarded to the finder. What is unusual about the remark is the possibility that something very much like this plan seems to have occurred in the original practical joke that provided a basis for the play.

In the letter from John MacPherson to William Patterson mentioned in the introduction, in which MacPherson names the real-life counterparts of most of the play's characters, the following curious sentence appears: "As to the play you spoke of, I take it to be *The Disappointment*, and can only say that it was well rec^d by the people here, who found no fault in it, but that it savored too much of partiality; as the Collector actually seized the Chest as the King's property, and, with a great deal of trouble, conveyed it on board a vessel then in the River, intending to send it home."

The comment on the reception of the play by the public must refer to the published version, inasmuch as it was never produced; but the reference to the actual seizing of the chest by the collector is obscure. Obviously, MacPherson is not referring to the action in the play, for the chest is not seized nor is it placed on board a ship. This seizure, if it took place at all, must have been part of the original joke, and in some way the collector in Philadelphia at the time must have been a part of the plot to humiliate the dupes, as he is partially involved in the play. The alternative interpretation of the collector's actions as described by MacPherson would make this important public official one of the dupes, fooled by Forrest and his friends into believing the treasure to be a real one. If this had been the case, it seems impossible that the resulting, inevitable public furor that would surround the discovery of the king's representative being hoodwinked would not become public knowledge and thus part of the annals of the period. I have found no mention of such an event in any other place but MacPherson's letter, and therefore conclude that the king's collector must have been involved in the plot as one of the perpetrators, if at all.

Lack of information makes the matter hopelessly confused; but the MacPherson reference is intriguing, when one considers the public pressures that were brought to bear on the production of the play.

72. "*One bird in hand.* . . ." An old saying, as Washball says, but one that is part of *Poor Richard's Almanac* and consequently very much part of the Philadelphia milieu. I have been unable to identify Washball's neighbor Symond, referred to in the next sentence. However, it seems likely, since the name is not a label-name, that such a person did live in the city at that time, and perhaps had a sign at his shop with at least part of the Franklin maxim on it.

73. "*Put the broad R on it.*" The reference is to the brand placed on goods and materials, particularly lumber, to identify it as crown property. Precisely, the brand was usually called "the broad arrow" or "the king's arrow," a description of an arrow-shaped mark made with a broadaxe on trees that would be reserved for use by the Royal Navy.

Act II, scene v

74. "*Nathing but staines.* . . ." The last word is McSnip's pronunciation of "stones." This line would not be as obscure to an audience as it might be to the

reader, as they would be aware of the contents as stones before McSnip spoke.

75. *"Dr. Witt's. . . ."* Dr. Christopher Witt, already referred to in note 59, was a well-known eccentric and scientific dilettante of the period. "At Germantown," say the Bridenbaughs, " 'facetious and pliant' old Dr. Christopher Witt, devotee of natural philosophy, physic, astrology and magic, divided his time between his library and his beloved garden" (*Rebels and Gentlemen*, p. 309). A contemporary called him "credulous" and concerned "much with the marvelous," as his interest in the mystical hermit Kelpius seems to indicate. Dr. Witt was not without friends, however, as we know Thomas Morrey willed a microscope to him in 1735, and he was probably suffered with a genial forebearance by the younger, more skeptical men of the community.

Precisely what tests Dr. Witt might have used to discover from Moll's urine whether she was a conjuror is unknown. Doubtless those versed in alchemy could extract volumes of information, and Raccoon has hit upon the person most likely to know this arcane art; but for us, the mystery remains.

76. *". . . the brig Welcome. . . ."* This is without doubt the only line given Meanwell that might have got a laugh from a Philadelphia audience. The brig *Welcome* was the ship that had carried William Penn to the colony in 1683, and was revered in the memory of the Pennsylvania Quakers as the *Mayflower* was to the Puritans. The laugh would have been one of recognition rather than of derision, and would probably have been meaningless to a stranger in the audience.

77. *Epilogue.* In the original edition, the lines in the epilogue are in italic, similar to the songs in the body of the play. This, added to the stage direction, *"Enter Hum singing,"* and the fact that the lines rhyme, suggests that possibly the entire epilogue was sung rather than spoken. If this was the case, it was unique and extremely innovative.

Bibliography

1. Baugh, Albert C., et al. *A Literary History of England*. New York: Appleton-Century-Crofts, 1948.
2. Bridenbaugh, Carl and Jessica. *Rebels and Gentlemen: Philadelphia in the Age of Franklin*. Oxford: Oxford University Press, 1942.
3. Brockett, Oscar G. *History of the Theatre*. Boston: Allyn and Bacon, 1968.
4. Churchill, Winston S. *A History of the English Speaking Peoples; The Age of Revolution*. New York: Dodd, Mead and Co., 1957.
5. Coad, Oral Sumner, and Mims, Edwin, Jr. *The American Stage*. New Haven, Conn.: Yale University Press, 1929.
6. Craigie, Sir William A., and Hulbert, James R., eds. *A Dictionary of American English*. Chicago: University of Chicago Press, 1942.
7. Dunlap, William. *History of the American Theatre*. 2 vols. New York: J. Harper, 1832; Burt Franklin, 1963.
8. Ewen, David. *American Popular Songs*. New York: Random House, 1966.
9. Fast, Howard. *The Crossing*. New York: William Morrow & Co., 1971.
10. Gagey, Edmond M. *Ballad Opera*. New York: n.p., 1937.
11. Hewitt, Bernard. *Theatre U.S.A., 1668 to 1957*. New York: McGraw-Hill Book Co., 1959.
12. Hornblow, Arthur. *A History of the Theatre in America from its Beginnings to the Present Time*. 2 vols. Philadelphia: J. P. Lippincott, 1919.
13. Kelley, Joseph J., Jr. *Life and Times in Colonial Philadelphia*. Harrisburg, Penn.: Stackpole Books, 1973.
14. MacNamara, Brooks, *The American Playhouse in the Eighteenth Century*. Cambridge, Mass.: Harvard University Press, 1969.
15. Miller, John C. *Origins of the American Revolution*. Stanford, Calif.: University of California Press, 1943.
16. Nettleton, George H., and Case, Arthur E., eds. *British Dramatists from Dryden to Sheridan*. Boston: Houghton Mifflin, 1939.
17. Nicoll, Allardyce. *A History of Early Eighteenth Century Drama, 1700–1750*. Cambridge, Eng.: Cambridge University Press, 1929.
18. *Norristown* (Penn.) *Herald*. March 23, 1825.

19. Odell, G. B. D. *Annals of the New York Stage*, vol. 1. New York: Columbia University Press, 1929.
20. *Pennsylvania Magazine of History and Biography.* 98 vols. 1887–1975.
21. Philbrick, Norman. *Trumpets Sounding: Propaganda Plays of the American Revolution.* New York: Benjamin Blom, 1972.
22. Pollock, Thomas Clark. *The Philadelphia Theatre in the Eighteenth Century.* Philadelphia: University of Pennsylvania Press, 1933.
23. Preston, John Hyde. *A Short History of the American Revolution.* New York: Bantam Books, 1953.
24. Quinn, Arthur Hobson. *A History of the American Drama from the Beginning to the Civil War.* New York: Appleton-Century-Crofts, 1923.
25. Rankin, Hugh. *The Golden Age of Piracy.* Williamsburg, Va.: Colonial Williamsburg, 1969.
26. ———. *The Theatre in Colonial America.* Chapel Hill: University of North Carolina Press, 1965.
27. Roberts, Charles. *A Generall History of the Robberies and Murders of the Most Notorious Pyrates.* London: n.p., 1724.
28. Seilhamer, George O. *History of the American Theatre: Before the Revolution.* Philadelphia: Globe Printing House, 1888.
29. Sonneck, O. G. T. *A Bibliography of Early Secular American Music (18th Century).* Rev. ed., edited by William Treat Upton. New York: Da Capo Press, 1964.
30. *South Carolina Gazette.* Charleston, October 30, 1766.
31. Southern, Richard. *Changeable Scenery; Its Origin and Development in the British Theatre.* London: Faber and Faber, 1952.
32. ———. *The Georgian Playhouse.* London: Pleiades Books, 1948.
33. Tyler, Moses Coit. *Literary History of the American Revolution.* 2 vols. New York: Putnam's, 1897.
34. Uden, Grant. *A Dictionary of Chivalry.* New York: Thomas Y. Crowell, 1968.
35. Watson, John Fanning. *Annals of Philadelphia and Pennsylvania in the Olden Time.* Philadelphia: n.p., 1823.
36. *Weekly Magazine.* Philadelphia, Penn., 1798.
37. Wilson, Garff B. *Three Hundred Years of American Drama and Theatre.* Englewood Cliffs, N.J.: Prentice-Hall, 1973.